HOMESICK

FINDING HOME WHEREVER YOU ARE

COME RISE WITH ME PUBLISHING

Hello@kayciaellingsen.com

Paperback ISBN: 979-8-9850980-1-3

Hardcover ISBN: 979-8-9850980-4-4

E-book ISBN: 979-8-9850980-5-1

Audiobook ISBN: 979-8-9850980-6-8

1st edition

Cover design: Britte Osiek

Edited by: Erika Harston Noll

CONTENTS

FOREWORD

I wish this book had existed when I was living sixteen hundred miles away from everything I'd ever known. I was in a completely different country and though I was with my husband and three children, I felt lonely and terrified for most of the time I was there. Things did not work out the way I had expected and having to move to and from a different country within six months was very traumatic. There was no guide on how to successfully transition into the unknown or how to successfully move back home...until now.

This book is a beautiful compilation of stories that will encourage any homesick heart. Moving to a foreign place, whether it's twenty minutes down the road or across an ocean, is often romanticized but the honeymoon period only lasts for so long. Eventually loneliness and loss creep in and if there isn't anyone in your life who can help you process it or get through it, the challenges can feel overwhelming.

This book gets high praise from me because it's a much-needed resource for anyone who has ever moved away and found themselves feeling lost and unsure. It's the kind of book that reminds you that there are many other people who have experienced the same thing and that you can, and will, absolutely get through it. I'm grateful to each of these courageous women for sharing their stories so vulnerably. This is the kind of book that can have a ripple effect that's felt around the globe.

Meggan Larson – Award winning and Amazon best-selling author, course creator, and authorpreneur.

BONUS COURSE

As a special *thank you* for picking up this book, here is *exclusive access* to the bonus course full of additional tips, strategies, and encouragement for movers!

HOMESICK

I knew immediately, but I lied to myself to pretend the pain would not get worse. "It's just a stomachache; it will go away." An hour passed, and there was no question in my mind that this was NOT a stomachache, but I still delayed calling her. "It's 2:00 a.m.; I don't want to call and wake her up at 2:00 a.m." By the time it reached 3:30 a.m., I had woken up my husband, who insisted that I stop delaying, so I did. Knowing full well that if she didn't answer, I had no one else to call, I picked up the phone and called a lady who had been a stranger to me six months before. It was another reminder of how far from home I was.

The reminders that I was on my own and didn't have local family or friends had a way of creeping into every part of my life. Even little questions got to me, like when I filled out the paperwork at the daycare. "Ah, I hate this question." I sighed and looked up from the forms I was filling out. I didn't have an answer. Should I leave it blank? Would they accept it? What if something actually did go wrong? I didn't have anyone in the whole state that they could call for help. "Well, I hope they don't ever need this information because I don't have an answer." I glanced down and reread the question.

"Who should we call in case of emergency if the parents cannot be reached?"

I sighed and drew a line through the blank where they wanted me to write the answer. It was those little subtle things that hit me. The questions I used to have no problem answering reminded me once again that I was far from home.

I was living the farthest away from home that I ever had. At first, I thought everything was good. I thought I would have no problem living here as I explored the new area excitedly. I enjoyed the new sights and places; however, the town's excitement and newness only lasted so long. I had done the local exploring, taken multiple trips to the park with my three-year-old, and found the library and walking trails. I had told everyone that I loved it and was thriving there. I had unpacked the boxes, set up our home, and settled into a new daily routine. After the chaos that goes with a move quieted down, *that* was when homesickness settled in. I didn't know if those feelings had been there all along, but once my world calmed down, my heart started calling for home.

The subtle call to go home hit me when I didn't expect it. It hit me on walks to the local story time alone with my daughter. It hit me during awkward conversations with people as I tried to juggle watching a three-year-old, figuring out *what* to talk about with complete strangers, and trying not to blush cherry-tomato red when I felt uncomfortable. The battle inside me raged between not wanting to have a conversation versus *needing* friendship. However, I needed to make friends more than I needed to feel comfortable, so I kept reaching for connection. At home, I journaled, filling the unwanted silence with written words. I wrote out the weekly highlights, what I learned from my bible readings, and my prayers as I had conversations with my only ever-present friend, God. I wrote prayers to find friends, belonging, and the strength to make it through.

I could feel homesickness weighing on my heart when I longed for face-to-face conversations with dear friends and when I heard strangers talk about visiting their parents for the weekend. I felt it when I desperately needed help keeping up with my three-year-old. It pulled on my heart when I least expected it, like when I was out at local events and saw groups of people laughing and having pleasant conversations. I quietly wished the people I cherished were closer. Some days my homesickness was soft and light, but other days, especially as the holidays approached, it was harsh and heavy. I didn't want to be homesick for the holidays; *I wanted to be home.*

There was no way we could fly our small family back home for two holidays in a row, especially since our daughter, Jada, had turned three, and we had to buy an additional ticket for her. "Do you want to go home for Christmas or Thanksgiving?" my husband asked me. "Christmas!" It was an easy answer, but I didn't know how much I would struggle with not being able to go to both. The thought of my extended family gathering without me brought me to tears. As the holiday grew closer, my homesickness grew, and the awareness that I was alone grew as well.

It was the first time I wouldn't be there. Our extended family gatherings were something that I looked forward to every year. Sixty people I love and cherish found a way to cram into one house. All the extra chairs were pulled out, and people filled every seating area. I looked forward to the warm hum of laughter, conversation, and the pitter-patter of kids walking around year after year. The hugs and jokes with cousins and making my way through the sea of family members to the buffet of Thanksgiving food and treats filled me with joy. It was all a stark contrast to our small family of three in our overly quiet and dimly lit apartment that felt *nothing* like home.

I tried to keep it out of my mind. It worked at first but became more challenging as the holiday decorations came out in stores, and the weather continued to cool. The dreary days felt colder when the holidays came up in conversations. The holidays had always brought me so much happiness, but that year, they brought my heart sadness. The tears would come randomly: at a stop light, walking my daughter back from the library, and many other times. The longing to go home would form a ball in my throat, threatening to remove the calm composure I strove so hard to keep. Then the call came.

It was an acquaintance we had met at church a few weeks before. "I know you don't have family in the area, and I was wondering - would you like to come over for Thanksgiving?" I held my breath as all the emotions I had been holding back wanted to spill over in that instant. "Yes. We would love to," I said through quiet deep breaths, giving it everything I had not to let the tears take away my ability to finish the conversation. After the call ended, I sank to the floor, thankful that we had somewhere to go for Thanksgiving and that God provided precisely the person I needed to make it through the holiday.

As the holidays passed, the warm weather swelled once again. This time my stomach was growing right along with the warm weather. I knew it wouldn't be long until I needed to call someone to watch Jada during the birth of our second child, but *I didn't have anyone to call*. Even though I had lived there for months, I didn't have friendships in the area. I had made a friend, but she moved out of state before the summer months were in full swing. After discussing the situation, my husband and I decided to take Jada to the hospital with us. If need be, Ethan would stay in the waiting room with Jada. We planned to do what was necessary to make it through, even if it wasn't ideal.

Then Friday, a day before my due date, as I picked Jada up from daycare, her teacher asked, "Who is going to watch Jada when you go to the hospital? If you don't have anyone, I will watch her." Relief flooded over me. How did I not think of that before?! I trusted her teacher, and Jada felt comfortable with her, too. "I would love that! We were going to take her with us to the hospital! So can I call you this weekend?"

"I have out-of-town plans this weekend, but I'll be back in town after Sunday." The stress I had just released climbed back onto my shoulders. "Oh, okay," I smiled and thought to myself, "Don't have the baby this weekend, don't have the baby on the due date." We exchanged numbers, and I walked out into the summer sun, knowing I still didn't have someone to call unless I could *somehow* make it through the weekend.

The phone rang once, twice, three times...

A quiet panic set in as I held my breath. "Who is going to watch Jada if she doesn't answer?" I realized at that moment that my backup plan of taking Jada with us to the hospital was horrible. "Do I have any other options?" I wished I had family or friends close by that I could depend on for help. "Hello," a groggy voice answered the phone. It didn't sound like her voice. Did I have the wrong number? I hesitated, "...Hey, this is Kaycia," but then was flooded with relief as the sleepiness left her voice, and I could confirm that I didn't call the wrong person! "Can you come to pick up Jada?" "Yes, where would you like to meet?" I hesitated again. Where should we meet? She had to drive into town, but from which direction? I realized I didn't know. Then I thought of

7

a place we were both familiar with - the easiest solution. "At the daycare?"

After the phone call, I took a deep breath of relief. In the nick of time, God provided the perfect solution to a problem I thought I couldn't solve. This woman was one of the only people my daughter knew in the area, and both Jada and I were comfortable with her! I was amazed at how God could provide the exact person I needed over and over again. Even when I felt utterly alone, He still provided.

Moving to a new area or state can be scary, especially if you do not know anyone around you. It is difficult not having a friend or family member to write down on the school/daycare emergency contact list, not knowing a single person in the town, and not being able to take a break when needed. Just because it is scary and difficult does not mean you can't do it. YOU CAN. Even if homesickness is heavy on your heart, God will provide a way for you to make it through. He can calm your anxious heart and help you make the right connections at just the right time.

ABOUT THE AUTHOR

"...once my world started to calm down in my new location, my heart started calling for home."

Kaycia is a wife, mom of three, moving coach, bestselling author, and course creator! She and her family have moved multiple times and have lived in 6 different states. Their latest move was less than a month ago! With all that moving experience, Kaycia teaches people who have moved to a new area how to heal homesickness by leading them through the process of creating friendships and excitement in their new location, *even if they are super shy!* Kaycia is passionate about continually learning and growing into the best version of herself. Adventure and stepping into completely new situations have become some things she craves, but it wasn't always that way. Her mission is to make sure you know you're

9

not alone in your journey and that you *can* create the life of your dreams!

FINDING MY NEW HOME

M y husband and I graduated from college on the same day. The next morning, we left our college home and made the long drive to California. My husband was going home, but I was going far away from everything I knew.

I was raised on a farm in a rural area of the Midwest. When I moved to the city to go to college, it was a significant change for me, but I was surrounded by excitement and fun, and all of us college students were in it together. I met my husband, Jason, in my second year, and we were married the following year. After being married for eighteen months, we had our first child. We graduated after another year of juggling classes, work, and our baby. We had settled into our little apartment and enjoyed hanging out with other couples attending the same school. After being in that city for five years, we were quite comfortable, yet ready for the next step in our lives.

My husband enrolled in an accelerated Master's Degree program in California, enabling him to finish the two-year program in one. This intense program meant he would be gone four nights a week, and since he would also be working full time during the day, he would not be home much, so we decided to move in with his parents, who lived an hour and a half from his school. We could save money, and I would have some companionship and help with the baby when needed. I was looking forward to getting to know my husband's family, and I did not realize how hard this move would be for me.

The first few months were the most difficult. Jason's brother and sister were also home from college for the summer, and our room was sandwiched between their rooms. The walls were thin, and we had to whisper to talk without being heard. We couldn't fit a queen bed in the room along with the baby's crib, so I slept on a twin while he slept on the floor next to me. Intimacy was challenging, to say the least. I had grown up with many siblings, so heading into that situation, I had thought it would be no big deal. However, I struggled with the lack of privacy.

We had been married and on our own for two and a half years, and it was a huge change to live in an extended family situation as a married couple; we had four generations in the home! They were always kind; my struggle wasn't because of anything they said or did. It was simply a situation that would have been difficult for any young couple. Aside from the lack of privacy, getting to know my husband's family was enjoyable. It was the first time I had spent more than a few days with them.

Getting around in the kitchen took some getting used to. I was constantly having to ask where things were while everyone else living there already knew. Compassionately, Jason's mom didn't ask me to take turns cooking regularly until Jason's siblings went back to school. This gave me a few months to learn the kitchen, but I was highly intimidated to cook for my husband's parents! I was still a novice and desperately didn't want to mess up. I had a list of recipes I knew how to make and was willing to learn new recipes, but there were some things I had not figured out how to do well yet.

Timing the different parts of the meal to be finished all at once was foreign to me, and it seemed like magic how my mother-in-law always had every part ready at the same time. I was also amazed that dinner was at the same time every day. I observed carefully for months and consciously practiced to learn to do it myself. I hadn't grown up with a set dinner time due to my dad's job and large family with many different commitments. We often started eating with part of dinner still cooking or just had to wait until the last item finished cooking. Learning to time everything was stressful, but I was determined to make the best of it. I saw this as an opportunity to learn something that would benefit my family, and I did my best.

My in-laws' house was meticulously clean, and they hadn't ever had a little child living there. Their children were grown, and they were empty nesters until their college-aged children returned each summer. I'm sure it was a big adjustment for them to have three of their children, a spouse, and a grandchild come live with them all at once. We babyproofed a few things when we moved in, like electric outlets and some cupboards for safety. But I still had to be very careful and watchful to ensure my daughter, who was just learning to walk, didn't get into any cupboards she shouldn't or break the beautiful glass items they had, like the Precious Moments figurines that filled a whole bookcase. She was very curious, and gratefully, my mother-in-law let her play in the Tupperware cupboard and use wooden spoons to pound on pots - which would entertain her at times each day when her toys had lost their appeal.

Since it wasn't our home, there wasn't a place for our things on the main floor. They gave us the bottom of the bookshelf for our children's books and a space on the counter for wipes and a couple of diapers. We also had my rocking chair, a toy basket, a baby swing, and a high chair. Everything else had to be kept upstairs in our tiny room. While we didn't have much (we had sold our furniture and many other things before we moved), it was hard not to have my things, especially all the baby's things, at my fingertips. I was still recovering from a back injury I had suffered eight months before, and up to that point, I had kept everything I needed close by because bending, lifting, and carrying my daughter was painful. Not having all my things readily at hand meant I had to carry her up and down the stairs multiple times a day.

I woke up every morning in pain, tried to manage as it steadily grew worse throughout the day, and many times at night, I cried myself to sleep as I prayed for relief from the intense throbbing. To make life easier and less painful, I compensated by making piles of supplies, baby clothing, toys, books, notebooks, and other belongings near my rocking chair or on the counters. These piles caused some strain, as they were understandably unwelcome, and I was often asked to clean them up. I know they didn't realize how much pain I was in because I had a cheerful disposition and didn't talk about it all the time, and I also never explained my reasoning behind the piles; I simply put them away upstairs when asked because I didn't want to cause problems.

Because of my injury, I was in physical therapy, and my doctor recommended that I do water aerobics as low-impact cardio to help strengthen my muscles. We only had one car, and my husband had it most of the time, so it was a blessing that we had a gym nearby. I looked forward to this time as it was one of the few things I could do independently. I would walk the few blocks regularly and put my daughter in the gym daycare so that I could attend the water aerobics class. I was hoping to meet some new friends

- peers - but they were all old ladies! Most young adults like me were doing more intense workouts that I could not do at the time. The instructor was great, the old ladies were sweet, and the class was just what I needed physically, but I was sad not to make any young friends as I had hoped.

I had even higher hopes of making friends at church, as having a common belief system is one thing that helps friendships go deeper. Walking in for the first time after our move was a homecoming for my husband. He was greeted warmly, and so was I, but after a little bit of small talk, most people turned and chatted old times with my husband while I felt like I was on the outside looking in. I felt this way for years with many of his friends. I didn't have a big connection with them like he did, and they would often talk about memories and past experiences, which meant that I couldn't participate in the conversations and we couldn't get to know each other better. Sometimes I felt mute because I just stood there smiling while everyone else talked about subjects I knew nothing about (on the bright side, listening to these conversations allowed me to get to know my husband better). The people were kind, but deep friendships take time, energy, and effort to build, and that includes balanced conversation where both parties get to speak, so I knew it would be a while before I had close friends.

It was easiest for me to connect with other moms who had little ones, as my daughter was eleven months when we first moved in. Thankfully, a few families in the congregation had children around her age, and I started building friendships. I was soon called to work in the children's ministry and got to know even more people. At that time, I didn't find a confidante or best friend, but over the next year and a half that we were there, I made friendships and began to feel like I belonged. I still keep up with some of those friends, even though I don't live there anymore. Attending church gave me a support system and opportunities to make friends that I wouldn't have had without it, and it helped with my feelings of loneliness since my husband was gone so much, and I was far away from my parents, siblings, and longtime friends.

In addition to being far away from many of the people I loved, I was also far away from the climates and plants I was accustomed to. It was not long before allergies hit me in a way I had never experienced before. I was itchy and swollen, and I couldn't breathe. I discovered I was allergic to several trees and grasses in the area that weren't as common where I had lived before. I loaded up on multiple OTC allergy meds to get by. As I continued to live in the same city, I searched for solutions to what became chronic bronchitis brought on by spring and fall allergies every year - I was physically miserable. Even my children's elementary school was surrounded by rows of a tree my body couldn't handle. During specific times of the year, every time I went to the school, I ended up in coughing and sneezing fits, no matter how many OTC or prescription meds I took. I finally found the answers I was looking for through friends who introduced me to holistic medicine and better nutrition. Thankfully, I overcame the chronic bronchitis that allergies had caused for many years. The path I chose for healing also helped guide me into my current career.

Being far away from everything I knew also meant I didn't know my way around the new city or surrounding areas, and I got lost several times, wandering around the meandering streets of the neighborhoods. Sometimes people assumed I knew where to go when I didn't. Once when I went to a neighboring city, I got directions that mixed up the mileage between turns. Following the directions, I accidentally went 10 miles out of the way, missed my turn, and ended up in Stockton. This was before cell phones and navigation. There I was, a midwestern farm girl, shaking in my boots as I stopped at a sketchy gas station and used a pay phone to call for help; yikes! Another time, I was driving home from another city with some friends and passed my freeway exit without noticing it because I was still unfamiliar with the area, although I thought I knew where I was going. We ended up over 20 miles farther down the road before we realized it. Thankfully, the detour wasn't a big deal, and we laughed all the way home, even though we were an hour later than planned. I learned to get the directions in writing, repeat them back to double-check their accuracy, and make sure I knew exactly where I was going beforehand.

I have lived in the same city for twenty-two years. My in-laws lived nearby for most of those years and supported our family immensely. My husband kept going to school for a while, continuing his education with several more degrees, and while it seemed like forever during those times, it was a small percentage of those years. I have had six more children since then and have moved to 5 different areas within the city. I have found friends I will be close to forever by going to the library, park, church, and my children's schools. I have met people who led me to the healing I needed. I have made this city my home and have loved living here. I have prayed, laughed, and cried as I have raised my family here. There have been tough times and extraordinary times, and I wouldn't change it for the world!

It may seem like it will never end when you face challenges, but those times don't last. You can make it through. Look for the positive, have a cheerful attitude, and try to make the best of your situation. Keep learning, pray often, rely on family, and seek solutions and new friends. Whether you stay for two years or twenty, finding home is about what's inside you, not the situations or troubles you find along the way.

"Whether you stay for two years or twenty, finding home is about what's inside you, not the situations or troubles you find along the way. "

Erika Harston Noll has had several health challenges that knocked her off her feet. Through the years, she has developed skills in advocating for herself and others, holistically supporting health with natural medicine and nutrition, and creating a healing home. Erika teaches other moms to do the same in her Facebook Group, Holistic Super Moms. Advocacy has become a passion project for her, and she enjoys helping others learn to advocate for themselves in many different situations.

Erika grew up in Illinois and is raising her family in California. She is happily married to her best friend, and they have seven children. Erika has a bachelor's degree in Comparative Literature, is a best-selling Author and Editor, is a Certified Nutritarian Coach, and has spent many years researching, implementing, and teaching holistic approaches to health as a Wellness Coach. She loves baking sourdough bread, preparing delicious plant-based meals, gardening, music, dancing, reading, homeschooling, and playing board games with her children.

TRUST YOUR JOURNEY

There was an emptiness and loneliness inside me that I couldn't shake or explain. I missed home more than I could have ever imagined possible. It wasn't a particular street address that I missed; it was the area where the majority of my family lived. I had moved a lot as a teenager and young adult, but this was different.

At 20 years old, I had been a single mother for three years, and my son's father had chosen not to be a part of our lives. I met a man at work, and he joined the military a few months after we started dating. His first set of orders was overseas. We wrote letters and talked on the phone as much as possible. He came back home midway through his overseas orders for our wedding. Our first set of orders as newlyweds were in Texas. I was nervous but excited to finally live together as a family and set up our first home together.

My husband went to Texas and acquired an apartment for us, and I put in my two-week notice at work. It was overwhelming yet exciting at the same time. I packed at least one box every evening after work starting with things we weren't using daily and wouldn't need in the next two weeks. There were moments of tears with me just sitting on the floor and staring at all the empty boxes waiting for me to pack them. I needed to have all but the essentials packed by the time my husband arrived so we could load up the truck and get on the road. Once my husband reached my home in Virginia, we packed the moving truck with all our physical possessions. I had a suitcase packed for my son and me with about a week's worth of clothes, hygiene items, and a small box of my son's favorite toys to play with in the car. My husband drove the moving truck, and I followed behind him in my car with my son. My heart was racing from excitement and a little fear of the unknown as we set out on our new adventure.

It was late in the evening as we crossed the Texas State Line. I began crying, and tears just rolled down my face from being exhausted from the hours of driving and the excitement of knowing we were getting closer to our new home.

We finally arrived, and I grabbed the box of my son's toys from the car. We went up the stairs to our second-floor apartment; it was small yet perfect for our first home. My son had his own room, and I was excited to unpack and set up our home. We began unloading the truck while my son played on the floor with his toys in his new room. Fully exhausted from carrying everything up the stairs, it was time to set up bed frames and grab the sheets from the box of linens to make the beds. At the very least, we had beds to sleep in once we finished unpacking for the day. I unpacked the towels and headed to the kitchen to unpack those boxes. We wouldn't be able to unpack everything in one day, but at least having beds made, towels to dry off from baths/showers, and the kitchen set up to prepare meals made it feel like home amid the unpacking chaos. After several days of unpacking, we finally settled into our new home.

Two months later, I was still desperately seeking a new job but had yet to be successful. I had excellent references and skills as an Administrative Assistant. Unfortunately, there were more people than employment opportunities in the area. I felt like a failure and that I had lost part of my identity because I was not able to find a job. I had started working at 16 years old, and aside from being a mom, work gave me a sense of purpose and worth in this world. It was important to me to get a new job and contribute to our family. I continued looking for a job and enjoyed the extra time with my son since he didn't have to go to daycare every day like he did when we had lived in Virginia.

Then I discovered I was pregnant; we were expecting our first child together. My son was excited to learn he would soon have a baby brother or sister. With another child on the way and a lack of jobs aside from retail stores or fast-food chains, my husband and I decided I would stay home and take care of our children full-time. Unless I found a good-paying job, two children in daycare would cost the same if not more than my possible earned wages. I wondered if I had made a mistake leaving my good-paying job.

The days started feeling longer, I began having trouble sleeping at night, and I would break down in tears during the day for little to no reason. I felt worthless being unemployed, but I pushed through every day to be the best mom for my son. I wondered how I would make it through when I was so far from my family.

One day while doing laundry at the apartment's laundromat, I met a neighbor who was also a wife of a service member with a young son. We quickly became friends. It felt good to have someone to talk to who understood how hard it was to adjust to this new lifestyle and area. It helped ease the loneliness I was feeling, and since she had moved there six months before me, she was able to share her knowledge of the area with me. I had always been more of an introverted person, so making new friends was challenging for me. I began going to her apartment every morning, and we would have coffee together while the kids played. We would run errands together with our kids, and the fog of loneliness began to lift a little.

A few months later, my husband introduced me to a fellow service member from his unit and his wife. His wife was born and raised in Texas, and they were also newlyweds. We became friends and would talk several times a week on the phone. I started talking to her about wanting to go home and see my family before the baby was born. One day I asked her if she would consider going with my son and me to Virginia. She said she had never left the state of Texas and seemed uncertain about the trip, but she talked it over with her husband and agreed to go with me. I quickly called my grandmother and asked if we could stay with her for a week, and she excitedly said, "Yes." I felt this strong urge to go home and see my family. I hoped I would find myself again and the trip home would help me feel better. However, my husband had concerns about me taking the trip.

I was six months pregnant and would be traveling with my son. He was relieved that my Texas native friend was willing to travel with me. I consulted with my doctor and was given the all-clear for us to travel. I was so excited and counting the days to see my family in Virginia again. It took us 24 hours straight to make our trip, only stopping to get fuel, use the restroom, and eat. My friend enjoyed seeing parts of our country she had never seen before. I was exhausted by the time we reached my grandmother's house, but I was filled with adrenaline and excitement to see her and hug her. I was finally home and at peace for the first time in months.

While in Virginia, I visited other family members and my mother-in-law. I was even able to take a day to relax at my grandmother's, watching all of our favorite shows together and showing my friend around the different places I had lived in over the years. I felt more like myself, the heaviness had lifted, and I was happy. That week passed way too quickly, and it was time to go home. I was excited to see my husband and show him all the gifts our family had given us for our unborn son. Yet a part of me wanted to stay near my family and familiar places. I realized some of the anxiety and depression I had been experiencing was knowing that my family wouldn't be close by to visit or to help when my second son was born. Suddenly it made sense why I had felt an urgency to be back around my family.

Three months after returning to Texas from my trip to Virginia, we welcomed our baby boy into the world. I was so excited about his arrival, and while I missed not having my family close by, we managed everything just fine. I was enjoying my growing family and had found a renewed sense of purpose and worth. My oldest son was always asking to hold his brother and offering to feed him his bottle. It was great having unlimited time with my children, even though there were days I still missed not having a job. Three months later, our lease ended at the apartment, and we found a house to rent in a nearby subdivision which gave us more room and had a yard for our kids to play.

One of my favorite memories was our first Thanksgiving in that house. I missed not being home for the holiday, so I asked my husband to invite all of the service members in his unit who were staying local to come to our house for Thanksgiving Dinner. My husband incredulously made sure I understood how many people were in his unit. I told him it was important to me, and since we couldn't be with our family, we would make a big family gathering with others who couldn't be with their families either. So my husband agreed. Around noon on Thanksgiving Day, people started arriving. We welcomed them into our home and directed them to the plates and food. Then as the first group of people left, more people arrived. We had a steady flow of people coming in and out of our home for several hours.

That evening a few of my husband's friends were still at the house, and I asked when was the last time they decorated a Christmas Tree. Most said it had been several years. I asked if they wanted to help decorate our Christmas Tree, and they agreed. So I quickly grabbed the Christmas Tree and decoration boxes and put on some Christmas music. It looked great, and everyone enjoyed being a part of our family festivities. That was such a fantastic day, and it provided the feel of a big family holiday despite being hundreds of miles away from our own.

After waiting almost two years, we finally received the call that base housing was available for our family. While living in base housing, we welcomed our third son into the world. I didn't experience the depression I had with my second son's pregnancy. This time, I felt more prepared and confident.

Less than two years after moving into base housing in Texas, my husband received new orders to Washington, D.C., and housing was already available for us in Virginia. It was super close to a large portion of my family! I could hardly contain my excitement and was counting down the days. That was by far my favorite move, and we did not even have to move ourselves. The moving company came and loaded up all of our furniture and boxes, and we were able to travel together in one vehicle, making it easier to tend to our children. Finally, I was going home!

Always trust your journey is for a purpose and that all of your experiences help you become the person you are meant to be. Your self-worth isn't tied to a job, and being able to be a stay-at-home mom is a blessing. The experiences you have give you the ability to help others that find themselves in similar situations. Mindset is extremely important and thinking about how even your darkest moments can be a guiding light to others is the most humbling and empowering feeling in the world.

Seek help when you are struggling with mental health. I waited years to seek help because of the stigma around mental health, yet once I went through counseling, it was clear how much the coping strategies would have helped me during those hard years.

"Always trust your journey is for a purpose and that all of your experiences help you become the person you are meant to be."

Michelle LeeAnn is a mom of five children, three boys and twin girls. She became a mother at 17 years of age. Michelle has endured judgment, struggled with self-love, and battled depression and health issues. It took her a long time to develop the mindset that she needed to be a warrior in a world full of worriers.

After several years of personal growth, she is a Certified Life Coach and Finance Coach. Her hobbies include exploring the outdoors, motorcycle riding, and gardening. In the colder months, you can find her curled up on the couch in front of a warm fire. She spends her time and energy creating a life she loves.

Finding Calm When Moving Brings Chaos

"What are we going to do?"

I slowly slid my back down the wall until I couldn't sink any lower. I pressed my palms into my eyes as I desperately tried not to cry. "Where are we going to live? We moved across the country for *this*, and our life is in shambles." This moving experience was supposed to be fun and exciting; instead, we ended up in chaos.

My husband and I had spent two years in Texas serving at New Life Church in Dalhart. When we first moved, we were filled with excitement. My oldest, Isaiah, was just two months old when we left our home in Wisconsin. Grace, my daughter, was born in Texas, and we served faithfully for those years with our little family. It was a fantastic place, filled with amazing people, but it never felt truly like home. The people and the climate were different and as wonderful as it was, living in the South wasn't a good fit for me. When my husband, Ken, told me we should move back to Wisconsin, it was the worst/best thing I'd ever heard. His dad was aging and needed help on the farm. Ken wanted to help, so we decided it was time to move back home.

On our last Sunday in Texas, the church hosted a going away party for us after the service. There was cake, time to mingle, and a small Dallas Cowboys piggy bank sitting on the counter next to the cake. "Leave a few dollars in the piggy bank if you want to bless Ken and Jess," our pastor said. We didn't think much of it at the time. We cried and said our goodbyes, reminisced about our time in Texas, loaded up in our Tahoe and U-Haul, and headed north.

About an hour into our drive to Wisconsin, Ken said, "Why don't you grab the piggy bank and see what we've got in there? Maybe we can use that to fill up when we stop next." I reached into the back, grabbed the piggy bank, and flipped it over to pull the stopper out of the bottom.

I was shocked when I saw that they had filled it to the brim with money. I looked at Ken and smiled as tears filled my eyes. He watched me questioningly as I pulled out the first bill - $100. I reached in and pulled out another - $100. I pulled and pulled and cried and laughed as we realized how much was stuffed into that little piggy bank. Bills and love notes with well-wishes packed that tiny thing, and I saw it for what it was: generosity from the kindest people we'd ever met. It gave me peace at that moment, as I didn't know what lay ahead, but I knew God had already provided for us.

When we got to the farm, it was a disaster. The bedrooms hadn't been opened or cleaned in a decade. We stayed for a few days with Ken's sister, but Ken was gone from morning to night as he attempted to help with the farm. After days of being alone, I finally decided we were going to be together. I loaded my two babies up,

Isaiah at two years old and Grace at six months old, and we moved to the farm.

I spent an entire day cleaning one room so we could set up a pack-and-play for the kids. The amount of stuff in each of the bedrooms was unreal. There was dust everywhere and spiders and spiderwebs in every corner. I used Clorox wipes to wipe the walls and surfaces, frantically working to gain ground while also occupying two little ones. It felt like trying to move a mountain with a garden spade. There weren't enough hours in the day for the work ahead.

On our first night at the farm, the coughing started. We used an old wood stove to heat the house, but there was no ductwork – so as it burned, much of its smoke rolled back into the living space. At first, the kids had a mild cough, and I didn't think much of it.

I spent the second day working on our room. I cleaned out all I could, and after an eight-hour day of cleaning again, I was exhausted. I listened as Grace and Isaiah coughed harder than before and started to get worried about what we were doing. Could we really do this? Could we live in this environment? I knew Ken's dad needed help, but was this where we were supposed to be? As my thoughts swirled, Ken slowly climbed the stairs and turned the corner. What I saw on his face stopped me in my tracks.

"Dad said he can't afford to pay me," he said. My heart skipped as I slowly slid down the wall to the ground. "What are we going to do?" We didn't have jobs – the *farm* was supposed to be the job. We'd moved our family across the entire country for *this*, and now his dad couldn't afford to pay him?

Chaos echoed in my mind as I decided how to respond. Before I opened my mouth, I paused as a wave of peace rolled over me. "God's got this," I thought. "He wouldn't have brought us this far to leave us." I was reminded of the peace I felt as we left Texas, that

33

deep well of calm that flooded my soul, knowing I didn't know what lay ahead, but I knew my God walked with me.

I also knew we needed to move in with my parents. Ken's dad couldn't afford to pay him, but my parents had a large home and had offered us space if we ever needed it, and at that moment, I could see the path ahead. We needed to move, but I didn't speak. Living on the farm was Ken's dream, Ken's call, and I needed to let him decide. We sat in silence, and I held his hand as he hung his head and sat in uncertainty. After the longest 20 minutes of my life, Ken lifted his head, looked at me, and said, "I think we need to move in with your parents."

My heart broke for him. He'd dreamed of helping his dad and bringing the farm back to life, and in just a few short days, that dream had been shattered – not from anything he had done, but simply because this path was not going to work for us and we needed to go in a different direction. The farm would be ok without us, continuing as it had before, but not with Ken as a part of it. I packed the kids up that night and left for my parents' house, still unsure of what lay ahead. The kids' coughs cleared up within the next few days, and that alone helped me realize we'd made the right decision.

As I drove away from the farm that evening, headed into the unknown, I heard that piggy bank rattle around as I turned a corner. That rattle was the ringing of peace. We'd left Texas with a plan for our future but no clue what lay ahead. God knew the moment we'd feel the earth drop out from beneath us and realize that we had no future on the farm. He knew the pain and the heartache we'd feel about the dream that we lost. He knew the fear we'd feel, and even without us knowing, God had already provided a way. The money from that piggy bank amounted to thousands of dollars, covering all our bills almost exactly until the paycheck from Ken's first job in Wisconsin was deposited. That money was dollars and cents, but it reminded us of love and support from people we'd only known for a short time in Texas but were forever imprinted on our hearts.

What started as a move with a clear path ahead of me quickly became a move filled with chaos. I felt doubt about our decisions, fear over my children's future, and agony over trying to protect my family while supporting my husband's dream. Despite all our best plans, moving from one place to another never quite turns out as we expect. In my situation, the ending was drastically different from where I started, but it wasn't a bad ending. The in-between was chaotic, but I found ways to sit in peace while it was happening.

I trusted God's plans for my life, which anchored me amid the chaos. I knew he wouldn't leave me, no matter how lonely I felt. I remembered and clung to the good things God had done in the past. I knew that the God who blessed us with thousands of dollars in a tiny piggy bank was the same God who knew the path ahead of us, even when the farm was not the right path. I decided I would be someone who remained calm and steadfast in the face of the storm, and I believe that you can, too.

When faced with uncertainty during your move, hold tight to the plans for your life. Cling to the good things you've seen before, and know that you can be rooted in who you are no matter what chaos the move brings. May you find yourself calm in the storm and sure as you step forward, walking boldly into the future.

"It gave me peace in that moment, knowing I didn't know the chaos that lay ahead, but I knew God had already provided for us."

Jess Kayhart is an author and speaker who loves to help others walk through difficult times. Drawing from experiences everyone can relate to, she encourages others to find meaning in the hard things and realize they can be OK right where they are. Jess and her husband live on an 80+ acre farm with their three children. She currently works as a Real Estate agent and serves as Worship Leader at the church in Reedsburg where her husband pastors. She has a master's degree in Theology, and her debut novel, *Father*

King, was an Amazon Bestseller. Jess looks forward to continuing to write, speak, and share her experiences to help other people.

FINDING THE COURAGE TO MOVE AGAIN

I wish I had an instruction manual on navigating the big moments in life. It would be visually represented in the form of a board game like Chutes and Ladders. When faced with an obstacle, all decisions would become multiple choice, and one would simply choose the path and carry on. Even when completely crushed and incapacitated by life, the board game would identify a step-by-step procedure for picking up the pieces. What a perfectly simplistic order life could offer, but that is a child's dream. As a military spouse, nothing in life feels stable. The military lifestyle often has individuals facing relocations, deployments, and isolation. I have been a member of this chaotic lifestyle for over twelve years and have learned many invaluable lessons along the way.

The spring of 2020 was a complete and utter catastrophe. The covid pandemic fabricated discord in the world that strained the already complicated logistical military movements to nearly impossible endeavors. My husband's assignment was in Montgomery, Alabama, and we were anxiously waiting to find out the location of our next assignment. However, a stop movement for military relocations caused a delay in all assignment notifications. For military families, anticipating an assignment to drop is like awaiting lab results from a health scare. The world had shut down, and there was so much conflict in society. On top of this, my alternating hormones and anxiety were at their height. I was eight months pregnant with my daughter, Callista. My son Atticus was about a year and a half old and could no longer attend preschool due to lockdown procedures. We also had no idea if my husband would be physically allowed in my birthing suite or if I would be an army of one because of increased safety precautions to minimize potential covid exposures. What would happen to the baby if I contracted covid? The unknown elements seemed to be ingredients in a recipe for disaster. Add a heap of chaos and a dash of confusion, then allow the pinch of a short timeline to get to a new location to bring everything to a boil. Voilà!

In general, relocation and the unknown are prevalent factors of the military lifestyle due to constant assignment transfers. Each relocation I experienced required a vast amount of bravery. Living all over the world may sound exciting and adventurous, but it comes with many obstacles. For starters, it was laborious to maintain and grow a career as a military spouse, and I was forced to sacrifice time with loved ones to excel in my profession. There have been instances where I wished I could flee to my hometown and spend time with my family, but instead, I lived in a location isolated and alone due to our careers. Also, as a spouse and parent, I had to determine if my occupation was worth the chase monetarily and mentally. It was also imperative to understand that I would not have the popular new-age motherhood "village" to help raise my family because of the frequent transfers. Luckily, I had close relationships with my parents and brother; no matter what, they were always just a phone call away. Knowing that gave me courage.

We finally received our Permanent Change of Station (PCS) orders for an assignment to Tampa, Florida, and we were in a pinch to arrive on time for our reporting date. Seven days after I gave birth to Callista, we packed up the cars and commenced our journey. The first few months in Tampa were a blur; I fully comprehended the gravity of recovering physically, emotionally, and mentally during the postpartum period and did my best to act accordingly. The number two was a common denominator in my daily life. I had two children under two years old, Callista nursed in two-hour increments, I pumped breast milk into two-ounce freezer bags every two hours, and I would return to work in two months. I felt like there was a short circuit in my body, and I functioned in a perpetual state of fight or flight.

Unfortunately, Callista had acid reflux causing colic, and I performed a series of rituals to get her comfortable for sleeping until her next feed and pump session. I would feed her, keep her upright for thirty minutes, burp, massage, and apply a warm washcloth to her abdomen. Some nights she would not let me put her down in the crib, and we would doze off together in the rocking chair until she woke again. On a good night, I would receive about two hours of uninterrupted sleep. While awake, I found ways to meticulously manage my time and utilize naps to unpack our household. My body was strained and pushed to the limit, and if there was an opportunity to rest, I could not turn my brain off. As a parent, I obsessed over extreme protective measures to decrease the odds of my family contracting the virus. I adopted a "not on my watch" mentality to keep my family safe at home.

Geographical distance from loved ones is another harsh reality of military lifestyle. Ironically, Tampa was the first location in twelve years that offered a direct flight back to my hometown, yet travel was not feasible. I longed for my parents to be able to visit and help out; however, my mother had an autoimmune disease that put her in the high-risk category, and we could not jeopardize her health. Instead, we continued to call each other multiple times throughout the day. We would joke that my parents were my kids' virtual babysitters, as they would entertain them through video chats when I needed a break. My mother would share advice, reflect on stories from my childhood, and make sure I was okay. She reminded me I would be okay and could make a home anywhere. Most of all, she would reiterate how proud she was and how much she loved me. That support meant the world to me.

About ten months later, life finally settled down and started returning to normal. It had been over a year since I last saw my parents, and I missed them tremendously. I was overjoyed that my parents were finally able to visit for Callista's first birthday. It was the first time they met her in person, and it was beautiful to hear them share feelings of love, laugh, and spend time together. At work, my career was accelerating, and I was accepted into a prestigious Department of Defense Leadership Program. Also, I created a book series that became a number-one international best seller. I received recognition and media acknowledgment in local, national, and international markets. And to top it all off, I was pregnant again with my second daughter, Ella. Everything was coming together, and I was happy.

Then it all fell apart. Shortly after her trip to visit us in Tampa, my mother's health began declining due to lupus. She spent months upon months rotating between the hospital and a rehabilitation center. Whenever my phone would ring or notify me of a message, I panicked and became worried immediately. I traveled to New Jersey several times to be with her and even witnessed gradual improvement. She was extremely loving and sweet; seeing her struggling was not fair. Mom knew of my pregnancy and was elated. Her goal was to get better for when her grandchildren would come and visit for Thanksgiving. She courageously battled lupus and put up a hell of a fight for her family. Then one day, her health took a steep decline, and she never recovered. Shortly after, I received the news that I had feared all my life. My mother passed away on November 2nd, 2021.

There are no words to fully articulate how grief feels. To say that my soul was heartbroken is an understatement. My sentiments of sorrow, anxiety, and depression were inexplicable. I often sat in silence in a state of shock as the world around me continued. I could not stop crying. Even while I was performing mundane chores, I wept. At night, I would reminisce on memories and imagine what it was like to be in her shoes. I would fall asleep crying. In the morning, I would wake up and panic once I realized her absence. I wanted to resign from my career. I could not talk to anyone about my grief without a complete breakdown, and functioning was arduous.

Amid my darkest depression, the military notified us we would be relocating to Okinawa, Japan, in the upcoming summer. The one person I wanted to share the news with and ask for advice was no longer physically present. If you have never experienced this level of longing for a person, let me tell you, it is the most gut-wrenching feeling in the world. I could barely force myself to leave the house; how in the hell was I supposed to move across the world? How was I expected to transport my three- and two-year-olds and my three-month-old baby to a different country? What about my elderly dogs? How would I find the courage to move?

To begin, I had to evaluate my life values. I figuratively picked myself up off the ground. My family has always been my number one priority. I focused on internal emotional healing and shed extraneous obligations. I ascertained that to be physically, mentally, and emotionally there for my family, I needed to start by preserving myself. I began to say "No" to obligations that would take away from time with my family. I used the time I gained to focus on my mental and physical health. I would take five minutes in the mornings to complete a guided meditation and physical activity. I made it a goal to get a walk in during the morning before the heat spiked. I am a true believer in the science behind walking and reducing anxiety. The amygdala produces anxiety and functions as a mono-tasker; in other words, it can only focus on one thing at a time, so when you are moving, your brain's focus shifts to concentrate on the movement. Also, there is a correlation between Vitamin D and mood elevation. Daily, I walked around my neighborhood and used the time to create calm and stillness in my mind. Over time, I felt calmer, stronger, and just overall healthier. This conscious self-care allowed me to have the energy to shift my mindset.

To find the courage to begin the daunting task of moving again, I contacted my friends who had previously lived in Japan and some who were currently there. I picked their brains and learned that the majority of them loved it. Next, I joined multiple social media pages and groups that were Japan-centric. I wrote down places to visit, restaurants recommended, and upcoming events that looked inviting. Then, I outlined a Venn diagram of the benefits and obstacles associated with the move. I revisited this list weekly to see if I felt the same. The more knowledge I acquired, the less taboo the move seemed. My list of obstacles eventually dissipated. Now that I was beginning to get excited, I was able to find the courage to execute the actual move.

I am more at ease and motivated when I have structure, especially when everything feels like it is inevitably crashing around me. Because of this, I made lists of what I needed to send to Japan immediately, items we required daily to live in a townhouse after the main pack out, and any imperative paperwork completion. Little by little, I chipped away at my lists. While completing tasks, I often reflected on my memories with my mother. I knew she would love for her grandchildren to be well-traveled and experience different cultures. I still missed her greatly and vowed to honor her legacy by living life to the fullest and teaching my children what she had taught me.

As I sit in my living room, watching my children play, to-do lists are hung on the refrigerator, classical music is playing, and I am reflecting on how far I have come. The tumultuous waves of uncertainty, doubt, and fear associated with the move have lessened. I was able to survive without my fictitious life instruction manual. I inadvertently created my own game plan to achieve a bit of solace. I did this by realizing that I have faced many of life's most significant obstacles and must give myself grace. I have learned that my values and priorities for my family have not nor will ever fall by the wayside. Overall, I understand and value that I am loved and never alone, even when I cannot physically see or hear my loved ones.

I would like to share one final affirmation that has brought me a bit of solace. A few weeks after my mother passed, my father found a quote that my mother had written that resonated with me. "The phrase, 'Do not be afraid,' is written in the Bible 365 times. This phrase is a daily reminder from God to live every day being fearless. Isaiah 41:10." I wish you courage, peace, and positivity with your move.

About the Author

"The phrase, 'Do not be afraid,' is written in the Bible 365 times. This is a daily reminder from God to live every day being fearless."
Isaiah 41:10

Athens E. Pellegrino grew up in Ocean City, New Jersey. She attended St. Joseph's University and obtained a Bachelor of Business Administration degree. Athens met her husband Christopher while attending the university and married in 2009. After, she studied at Troy University and received a Master of Public Administration degree. Athens serves as a Budget Analyst and military spouse in the United States Air Force. She has a love for traveling, cooking, dogs, and fitness. Athens and Christopher have a son, Atticus (age 3), and two daughters, Callista (age 2) and Ella (3 months). The family has experienced 8 Permanent Change of Station (PCS) assignments. Athens is intrigued by the strength and resiliency of military families, which led to her creation of the

Military Child Chronicles series. The first book is *Mission: My First PCS* followed by *Mission: Mistletoe.* She was most recently recognized as the Armed Forces Insurance MacDill Air Force Base Military Spouse of the Year 2022. Athens and her family are currently relocating to Okinawa, Japan.

Our Foundation Shook, But it Did Not Break - A Story of Love, Loss, and Growth

I will never forget the moment I approached my newlywed husband and asked him if we could move to Chicago. He was lying on our bed in his pj's, relaxing. I had been nervously rehearsing in my mind all day how I wanted to bring it up. Of course, it came out nowhere near how I had rehearsed. "What do you think about moving to Illinois?" I blurted out. The look on his face when he glanced up from his phone will FOREVER be ingrained in my mind. It was a mixture of utter surprise, excitement, and curiosity. "Um, really?" he responded. "Sure," I said. "Why not?"

You see, my husband and I had been married for approximately two months, and three things prompted me to ask this big, life-altering question. First, my husband had a bachelor's degree with science specializations, and he could not find a local job that was right for him. He was working at a job that paid the bills but did

49

not make him happy, and his salary was not good. Second, we had visited his brother and partner in Chicago a year earlier and absolutely loved the city! Third, we were young with no children or pets, perhaps a bit naive, but ready to explore the world and go on our first adventure as husband and wife!

I continued to probe him with the idea. I told him we had our wedding money that we could live on for a while until we found jobs. We didn't have a lot of stuff, so packing and moving would not be that bad. It was the perfect time to go for it. He just looked at me like I was crazy. So, I ended the conversation with, "Well, why don't you just think about it, and we can talk later." We left it at that.

Two days later, my husband brought it up. He said we should seriously think about it. So, we decided to take another trip there to see if we still loved it the way we did before. We walked around Chicago for hours, talking about the "what ifs" and pros and cons, and then we both stopped and just looked at each other. We knew what the other one was thinking. We started looking for apartments that afternoon. We decided if we got approved for the specific apartment we wanted for the month we wanted to move, we would sign the lease papers immediately and figure things out as we went. Within twelve hours, we received the news our application was approved, and we signed the lease agreement. We were moving to Illinois! We are firm believers in signs. When God opens a door, you walk through it. I will always blindly and faithfully walk through it and know things will fall into place as they are meant to be.

Neither of us knew what we were getting into and certainly did not foresee what would soon unfold. We did know that we loved each other and were ready for a big change. We had both lived in South Dakota our whole lives, and we knew our parents would not be happy about this. We were both a momma's girl and a momma's boy. We traveled back to Sioux Falls and told our family and friends that we were moving in only three months! One of the hardest conversations I have ever had with my mom was telling her I was moving away for the first time and that I was the one who got the ball rolling on the decision.

The time came, and our family packed us up in a tiny U-Haul trailer and our vehicles. We shed so many tears, and I started second-guessing our decision. I cried for two hours after we left but started getting more excited as we got closer. We were really doing this!

I'm a very positive, upbeat human, but also a very socially awkward introvert, and so is my husband. We had no idea how we were going to make friends. With no children or pets to use as a buffer, making friends was all on us, which scared us half to death. When our apartment community had social events, we would hype each other up, attend the events, then sulk back to our apartment because neither of us was brave enough to talk to anyone - this happened countless times.

I was offered a job, started within a month of moving, and began making friends through work. Charlie continued to apply for jobs, and everything seemed to be going great. But, as time went on, things started changing. We both felt a significant strain on our marriage. We missed our family, and Charlie was still unemployed. I remember coming home one day, and he was sitting there - something was definitely wrong. That afternoon he told me he wanted a divorce.

The combination of getting married, leaving the only place and people we knew, and being unemployed all in eight months caused him to become depressed, according to the marriage counselor we started seeing. We still loved each other very much and were trying desperately to navigate it all. We fought for our marriage. Every day, we practiced listening to understand, not just to respond, over and over again. We took a step back to understand each other's point of view, and no matter how much we disagreed on a particular subject, we did our best not to talk over each other. Being a newly married couple, learning and implementing each other's love languages was also a huge, positive turning point in the health and foundation of our marriage. It took time, work, and therapy, but we didn't quit.

When one of us was weak and on the edge of giving up, the other mustered the strength and pulled the other up. This back-and-forth lifting happened countless times. I am not going to sugarcoat it; it was tough. We had to work on our verbal communication, be aware of our nonverbal communication, and never assume we knew what the other person wanted or needed. Several people close to us suggested we quit and move on. However, they forgot how stubborn we were and that we were not about to quit just because things got hard.

During our struggles, Charlie finally landed a job he absolutely loved! I was still loving my job. We began making friends with other couples through work, and things started falling into place. The good times started to outweigh the bad. The strong foundation we had been so desperately working on was finally holding us up.

After two tough years, we were in a great place in our marriage, ready to buy a home and start a family. Then tremendous heartache hit. We were diagnosed with unexplained infertility. We did every test imaginable, and they could not find anything medically wrong with either of us. My Ob-Gyn referred us to an amazing fertility specialist close to our new home. Then a HUGE God wink happened, as Illinois has state-mandated infertility coverage. Without that financial assistance, we would have never been able to afford all the testing and procedures ourselves. We had two IUI procedures that both failed. The emotional turmoil and stress on our marriage were again in full force. However, this time we had a strong foundation. Did it shake? Sure, it did - we are human, after all! But it did not break.

Our fertility doctor sat us down and told us it was time to start considering doing IVF, in her professional opinion. We had a huge decision to make. Were we going to try IVF? What if it did not work? What would it do to my body? At first, my husband and I were not on the same page. I remember the endless nights I would cry myself to sleep, wondering what the right decision was and if we would make it. Reluctantly, my husband agreed with me, and we started the process of IVF. It was a very emotional process involving many injections and medications. My husband had to do injections for me because I was not good with needles! We ended up with six embryos and decided to implant two and freeze the others. The IVF procedure worked! One of the embryos split, and we became pregnant with triplets! We were overjoyed, and everything seemed to fall into place again.

Then I went in for a routine ultrasound visit and heard the words no pregnant woman ever wants to hear. Two of our babies did not have a heartbeat. Since we had so many IVF appointments and had to choose which ones my husband would take off work for, I was alone that day. I sat in the waiting room after the appointment, staring at the wall. I didn't know how I was going to tell my husband. One of the nurses came out and said nothing but just hugged me and let me cry on her shoulder. That comfort was exactly what I needed.

We were still pregnant with our little miracle jelly bean, as we called him. We had made an army of supportive friends, even being socially awkward humans as we were. They surrounded us with so much love and support.

We already loved our little miracle jelly bean so much, and everything was going great. Then the unimaginable happened. While I was home alone, I started getting terrible pains in my stomach. Everything got blurry, and I do not remember much. I gave birth to our son, Jaxson Dean, at home, and he was much too young to survive. Later, we found out my uterus lining had a microscopic tear in it, which caused him to be born early.

After losing Jaxson, time seemed to stop for me, and it felt like I was walking through a haze that no one else could understand. I could not sleep, and I did not want to eat. Nothing seemed to matter anymore. All I wanted to do was hold our son again. I rarely left our house because seeing couples with babies was too much for me. Isolation was much easier than seeing the look on people's faces when they saw me. No one knew what to say, and honestly, neither did I. As the world kept going, mine seemed to have stopped, and I had no idea how to move forward.

While all this unimaginable tragedy and extreme heartache were happening, the Lord was working in the background. He knew we now desperately needed our family; I needed my mom. A newer lab had opened up in our home state. My husband got a fantastic job offer doing what he loved there. It was time to close the door in Chicago and walk through the new door the Lord had opened.

We started this journey as a young, naive newlywed couple looking to explore and have our first great adventure. We took a chance, and we grew and evolved as a couple. I wholeheartedly believe life is meant to be lived. I will always recommend making the move, taking the chance, and following your heart and opportunities as they come. No one told me how hard it would be, and I am sure I would not have believed them if they had. The biggest lesson I learned was that you do not have to have it all figured out. Take one day at a time and be present in the moment. "Do not borrow worries" is a quote my mom taught me during that very difficult time, and I carry that with me wherever I go. Do not dwell on "what ifs," and certainly do not worry about the "could have beens." We experienced so much love, loss, and growth in this first chapter of our lives together, and our next chapter was soon to begin.

"When God opens a door, you walk through it. I will always blindly and faithfully walk through it and know things will fall into place as they are meant to be."

Alicia Williams is a wife of 14+ years, an angel mom, an IVF warrior, a content creator, and a business owner. Alicia and her husband have lived in four states and seven cities. The last big move was two years ago.

A former early childhood educator of 19+ years, she is now the owner of Babb's Blessings, which she created to keep her mother's legacy alive. It is an online shop where you can purchase special bundles and boxes for different occasions or just to let people in your life know that you are thinking of them. She has a very soft place in her heart for specializing grief bundles and bundles for couples going through fertility treatments. It is truly a legacy of love.

Alicia has an addiction to traveling and learning all about different cultures. She loves being in nature, and the ocean is her favorite place to be. She loves staying active; her favorite outdoor activities are hiking, snorkeling, and boogie boarding.

She is very close to family and friends in her home state and travels back to South Dakota whenever possible. She especially loves to love on her nephews and niece. She believes life is meant to be lived and experienced to the fullest. She is definitely a cup-half-full gal with a genuine love and passion for people and life.

GOD'S LOVE LETTER

We moved 2,200 miles to a place we had never been with no connections nearby. In a way that only God could orchestrate, our family's collapse to rock bottom allowed us to start a new foundation built upon His promises. This orchestration is just one of the countless reasons I call our story "God's Love Letter," and I desire to inspire hope and encourage you on your journey.

Few people would say they had the best year in 2020. We were struggling through the state-mandated destruction of our small business, unimagined financial strains, the depression and anxiety of essentially being on house arrest, and the infection of fear the world was fighting. The feeling of being trapped hit my fiercely independent nature especially hard.

I have always highly valued independence. Let's jump back to age seventeen when I left Oregon for college in Idaho and found the love of my life, James. Ready for our next life adventures after college, we began traveling. Moving was such a massive part of our lives that by our late thirties, we had lived in forty-three states between us!

Years later, when we finally felt the urge to settle down, we opted to move near my family in Oregon. Despite my amazing experiences and the connections I felt to many of the places I had lived, I was an Oregonian through and through. I wanted to buy a home and live out my life in the place where I had formed so many of my very best core memories. I thought I was going home for good, but God knew it wasn't final.

We spent years in Oregon working hard, saving money, and preparing to live out the next chapter of our American Dream in a home of our own. We finally found ourselves with a down payment in hand, making offers on homes, only to watch them stay just out of reach. Our discouragement was mounting as we made offer after offer over several years.

I sank deep in reflection and prayer and broke down in tears more than once. Many times in those years searching for a home, I cried out and asked God to please bring us the desire of our hearts. We had all the pieces the world told us we needed; a good-paying job, business, and friends and family nearby. *So why did our dream stay out of our grasp?* We desperately clung to faith, but if I am brutally honest, I felt myself slowly giving up.

I could feel the grief, or maybe fear, taking hold deep in my heart that we would never be able to buy our own home and live the life of our dreams. In our increasing desperation, we thought the practical thing to do was to reset our expectations. In a conscious downgrade from the hobby farm we desired, we decided to *settle* for just a house. After all, we were first-time home buyers!

Firmly planted in my scarcity mindset, I vividly remember the sting of pain when someone described how great it would be when we got our "little farm." I was on track with *my* plan for my life, so why wasn't that little farm coming? So there I was: strong-willed and stubborn, and this dream became the place God needed me to surrender completely.

It may be the pictures in our head of how we think life is supposed to be that screw us up or cause us to become stuck when things don't happen as planned. For our family, hitting possibly the deepest and darkest place together finally shook us from being "safe" (and stuck) where we were. God was calling us to something entirely different from the ideas we had settled into, and we had been too comfortable to hear the call. Perhaps I was too focused on what *I* wanted or on *my* vision of my life, but God had other plans.

While I didn't give up on knowing God would provide, I had to release my natural tendency to want to control things and know how they would turn out. It sounds silly seeing it written out. *As if I knew better than God what should happen in my life and when.* Thankfully, as I was learning to let go, God was preparing a life bigger than my dreams and better than my limiting beliefs would have allowed me to build on my own.

The final straw eventually came in the 2020 "pandemic" with Oregon's rapid loss of freedoms. We lost the right to travel, shop, work, and ultimately provide for our family. Rock bottom was having the government proceed to destroy the business in which we had invested not only our financial nest egg but our blood, sweat, and tears. I was outraged over the separation from our family as our governor decreed who could and could not gather in our private homes to celebrate our holiday traditions. We were forced to gather in secret and hide in a way no one should ever have to experience.

We decided that we couldn't continue to *live* in Oregon. How could this be the life of *free* Americans? We felt like outsiders living in some alternate reality. This place was no longer our home, and we decided not to tolerate it while we had the power to make a change.

That summer, my husband and I brought ourselves to ask, "Where would we go if not here?" I was surprised at what I heard. When I asked James where else he would consider living, almost without hesitation, he answered, "Missouri." I was stunned. It was one of the few states I had never visited, and my brain went to some terrible desolate version of high-plains, dustbowl-type flatland. I quickly blurted out, "Why Missouri?"

Years prior, we wouldn't have been ready or open to starting again in Missouri because James had sworn off returning to the Midwest after his childhood there. But in contrast, he told me how positive his experience was living specifically in Missouri years before. In September 2020, despite the many travel restrictions still active at the time, God provided me with an opportunity to travel there and see it for myself. Much to my surprise, I found the Ozarks were in stark contrast, in the best ways, to what my brain had initially envisioned.

Now we had to make the idea of escaping this life that had become so foreign in Oregon into a reality and see what God had for us as he opened this door to move one last time!

Financially, it hardly seemed like the appropriate time to up and move as our savings were dwindling. We had lost our business and its income, and my healthcare IT contracting work that had steadily flowed without interruption for the seven years prior was completely dried up. I was ashamed that I had gone from being a fully independent professional woman to needing to apply for unemployment. I was so embarrassed that I couldn't provide for myself for the first time in my life. As I surrendered to the outside support our family needed during this time, God was teaching me to depend on Him.

God was faithful in His perfect design and timing. My unemployment expiration came the week before I secured work at the start of 2021. I could not have planned that transition after so many months out of work, but God could. *But what about our business?*

The financial losses we incurred by closing our Oregon business generated a tax refund large enough to replace the home down payment we took out of savings while we fought to stay afloat during the prior year's collapse. By moving to a state with a lower cost of living, we could buy an entirely different home (and land) for the same price as a small cookie-cutter starter home in our former neighborhood.

Let's face it - we weren't getting any younger, so we just skipped the starter home and moved to our forever home! Chalk it up to just another area of my life that didn't comply with the "norm." That was such a blessing because God's version was much more glorious than fitting into this world!

I snapped a photo of my vision board on Dec. 30, 2020, as we were packing to flee Oregon. On it was my placeholder dream home, the image that allowed me to see an exciting future and visualize myself living there. It was white with multiple stories, lots of windows, and a big front porch set against a tree line. I shared pieces of this story on my blog and showed a close-up of two images – my vision board home and our real home in Missouri. I hope you will connect with me there to see the photos and witness what God provided for us!

I could spend an entire book telling you the intricate and caring details God had perfectly woven together to lead us to the home He had prepared for us and heal our homesick hearts. *I would scarcely believe the story myself if I hadn't lived it!* And as we chose to step out in faith and obedience to God's calling, out of our darkness, we found such great favor.

On the surface, we found our rural homestead dream, and our preparations to create a self-sufficient life came to fruition. We experienced gardens overflowing with abundance in the same growing season when others in our region experienced complete loss from heat and drought. We even adopted our dream dog, who had previously lived only on my vision board!

As we rebuilt our businesses in Missouri, we found clients who were so closely aligned with our personalities that we quickly became close friends. Financially, we started new income streams and received other windfalls that we would have never imagined, allowing us to rebuild and succeed in our new life in Missouri.

We found a place to build community for our family and others; a place of safety and tranquility that was truly therapeutic. Through intentional investment in relationship-building, we made many friends, close neighbor connections, and homesteading networks. The new communities we built abundantly blessed us.

Above all, we found such peace, joy, and freedom. We may have moved to S. Ridge Road, but our homestead stood atop what we claimed in His holy name as Freedom Ridge!

Looking back at my dream board, I see several text phrases that inspired me. The one glued on the edge of the house picture said, "ESCAPE the ordinary." Other text quotes around the home image were: "Best Times," "Amazing Things WILL HAPPEN," "Wildly Good," "Dreamer," "Grateful for Support," and "Wild & Free." That was the space I was in as I prayed for these blessings. I invite you into that same space, fully surrendering your need to know what your move will look like as you keep your eyes focused on Him.

I've heard so many times that I was *lucky* for the things in my life. In reality, that couldn't be farther from the truth! I have been walking with God in this great adventure, most recently living out His love letter for our move; that is my game-changing strategy. You are called to the same, my friend! God is inviting you into His purpose for your life; His calling for your future. There is an abundance that comes when living out your adventure life.

Whether you're moving due to loss or opportunity, I implore you to write that next great chapter in your life story along with the Author of Life. May you come to experience His peace, richness, and pure love that is unlike anything else.

"Trust in the LORD with all your heart, And lean not on your own understanding; In all your ways acknowledge Him, And He shall direct your paths." Proverbs 3:5-6 NKJV

You will find home somewhere you feel free. That is where you belong, my friend.

ABOUT THE AUTHOR

"Thankfully, as I was learning to let go, God was preparing a life bigger than my dreams and better than my limiting beliefs would have allowed me to build on my own."

Echo Alexzander is the Chief Adventure Officer of her brand, Adventures for #RealLife. Adventure is, of course, her life word. She was prophetically named to be an echo of the voice of the Lord and share her Christian faith with the world.

A wife and entrepreneur, Echo and her husband James live on their dream homestead in the Ozarks, in southwest Missouri, USA. Echo speaks life and seeks to build community while teaching about freedom. She considers herself an American patriotic activist and US Constitutionalist. She teaches about travel, wellness education, and personal growth to help create more fun, health, and overall abundance in the lives of others.

Echo loves authenticity, and her goals include bringing a new revolution of love, abundance, and integrity. She is leaving a legacy never to forget this wisdom and for it to echo for generations.

She's also hustling daily to make unicorns admire her as much as she admires them!

Moving to America, Where the Streets are Paved with Gold

"Hey, a lady wants to take you to America."

Those were the last words my headmaster told me when I was in the orphanage. It wasn't long before I made my way to America. I was super excited, anxious, and homesick, partly because I had left my brothers. But I didn't let anything get in my way because I wanted a better life. Every time American missionaries came to the orphanage, I eagerly went to them and stayed with them, practicing my English. I was in love with the missionaries and craved the special kind of caring atmosphere they carried with them. I couldn't believe I was going to America, the land where the streets were filled with gold.

That's what I thought. My flight was very long; it was about twenty-four hours from when I left Nepal to when I landed in America. I watched my first American movie called, "Snow on

Cedars." I didn't understand 90% of the English that they were saying. I imagined what they were saying. I cried throughout the movie because it was a love story. I didn't want to forget the movie title, so I memorized it. Many years later, after I was married, I decided to rewatch that movie, and let me tell you something. It hit me so hard. I felt like I was back on the airplane. I relived it all over again, and all the things I had imagined about the movie were right. I couldn't believe my luck.

After we landed at the airport, Kamron, the lady who brought me to America, bought me a Sprite. The taste and smell were so new and distinct that, to this day, Sprite is my favorite drink. It brings back a lot of memories, including staring at people in the airport. Kamron had said, "Ok, now in America, we don't stare at people. It's very rude." Instantly, I looked the other way, but I couldn't help staring. I had never seen so many tall people, let alone people riding on fancy cars. That's what I thought at the time, but now I know they are called wheelchairs. I also saw extremely obese people for the first time in my life. I definitely had culture shock. As we were walking, people kept getting on the moving walkways where they just stood, and it took them wherever they wanted. I thought it was magic, and the people were floating.

After we got to Kamron's home, she introduced me to her family, who were very sweet. Her kids were kind to me; however, the older one was distant. I can only imagine her feelings, and I didn't blame her one bit. The other two girls loved me. The middle child was a sweetheart, kind, generous, and truly cared for me. The youngest girl called me "sister." I had always wanted a little sister; I couldn't believe my luck. I had two little sisters and one big sister. We would play outside for hours and visit the neighbor girls. They were also very kind to me.

The family's dad was honestly my favorite. He was a good man. The minute he laid his eyes on me, we connected. I knew in my heart he loved me as his daughter, and I felt safe with him. Whenever I missed home, I would find him wherever he was. He would speak in a way I felt loved. The mom was kind and sweet as well. We bonded right away, but then months went by, and I'm not sure what happened, but the mom started to get distant. I have no idea to this day what I did wrong. I knew things were bad when I didn't hear my name called down in the mornings. I would sit on the steps and listen to their laughing coming from their parents' bedroom.

After eight months with that family, we went to their friend's house for dinner. While I don't remember all the details, I remember my feelings that day. We ate on the porch, and it felt very set up. One thing you must know about me is that I can sense things. I am very intuitive, perhaps it's a mechanism to survive whatever is coming my way, but I knew something was happening. They told me I was going to sleep over. I sat on the bed, and this lady named Marie gently told me why I was at her house.

We had crossed paths before. In 1998 Marie came to visit the orphanage. We all fought to sit by her because we thought she was a princess, perhaps even Diana. She was so beautiful, especially in the way she loved all the kids she had never met. Her kindness had always stayed with me. So as I sat on the bed, she showed me all the beautiful clothes, new bedsheets, and bunk bed she had bought for me. She told me I was not going back. Her home would be my new home. She said a lot that I don't remember. However, the words that stood out to me were, "Now I know they changed your name from Kripa to Kristi. Do you want me to call you by your new name or Kripa?" I told her Kripa would be nice. Then

71

she said, "You can call me grandma, aunty, or mom. You can call my husband Dan, grandpa, or dad."

I decided to call her mom because she was way too pretty to be called grandma, and I had never met my biological grandparents, so I thought it would be bad luck to call them grandparents. I called Dan Papa because calling another man dad, I thought, would be more bad luck. When my mom left the room, I lay on the soft bed and cried so hard that I wished I could return to Nepal. I had had enough of this and wanted my brothers, who were still at the orphanage. I was their protector, and I had left them behind. I felt so much pain and guilt at the time. My eyes were red from crying, and I was angry with myself. Sometimes I still feel that way. It's not fair that I have this life, and they can barely find a job to support themselves. I was full of sadness, and I felt betrayed and heartbroken. I loved having little sisters and missed them. It's one of those memories that comes and goes, and maybe someday I will see them. Perhaps I can say "Thank you" for being a part of my adoption story - I would never have made it to America if it wasn't for that family.

From the moment I lived with my new family, they were kind and loving. My dad worked in the city, and my mom stayed home with me and did side work. She would teach me English all day and correct my grammar. Sometimes I would get so upset with her that I wouldn't talk. I still remember when she taught me how to say "fish." I would say, "fiss."

My mom would say, "Kripa, try saying it like this, "Fi...sh..." I immediately regretted speaking. Another word was "pizza." I would say, "pijja." To this day, my mom corrects my grammar, and seven more people have joined in correcting me - my husband and children.

Then we moved to a new home a few hours away. The move itself wasn't hard for me at all. I had moved my whole life - what was another town? As we drove to the country from the city, I gazed through the window, "This is it. I move again. I will be ok." We drove for three long hours, and with my car sickness, it felt like we were driving for days. Between bathroom breaks, grabbing dinner, getting gas, and listening to the radio, we finally arrived. There were no houses, and the scenery was filled with trees. Our house was in the middle of nowhere. There were no neighbors; it was just me, my mom, and my dad. That's it. No cars driving. No other human beings. Our closest neighbor was about a mile away, but not the friendliest.

The move may not have been hard, but I missed my only friends. At first, it was hard and lonely, but hey, at least I was surrounded by trees. That summer, I walked up and down the driveway. I didn't see people for so long. I would talk to myself - I was bored out of my mind. I made up so many stories in my head and had imaginary friends. But the next four years were some of the best years of my life. I met many wonderful people in high school; some are friends for life, even though I live far away from them. My school bus would come straight to my front door. I felt special, but the truth was that the bus driver didn't have a choice.

I made friends with all kinds of groups. No one told me every-one hung out with their own particular group. One day I would hang out with the popular kids, and the next day with some awesome geek friends. I tried hanging out with the math league a couple of times; however, I didn't pass with that nerdy group. I tried everything. I wore nerdy high pants and glasses and even carried books to look smart. But I didn't have enough of the nerdy vibe. One of my best friends from high school introduced her cousin to me at a wedding. Who knew I would end up being her relative?

Before I knew it, I was in college working towards my AA degree and trying to find out what I wanted to do for the rest of my life. I would often think about Nepal. I would dream about Nepal. I wanted to choose a career that would help other people. That was always my goal - to come to America, get my degree, and become someone so I could return to Nepal and help poor people. After marrying my friend's cousin, I became pregnant. My husband and I had our daughter, and I attended college at night. When I was away from my daughter several times a week, I would sit there during class crying because I missed my baby. After two weeks of school, I told my husband I couldn't do it. I wanted to be home with my baby. The thought of leaving her for a couple of hours a night just about killed me. That was twelve years ago, and I am still home with my babies.

Many people ask me, "Don't you miss your family? Don't you miss Nepal? How can you live here and not think about your family?" Of course, I miss my family. I don't ever see my biological mom or my brothers. I believe our brains don't allow us to open that "box," at least not daily. What I mean by that "box" is our hidden traumas. Sometimes I think about my family, and I cry until I have no tears left. The thought of not seeing my brothers hurts deeply, but this is what I know: I have a good life here. I can be somebody here and stay home with my children to raise them. I have a husband who loves me for who I am, and he provides. I wouldn't have this life if I were in Nepal. It is one of the poorest countries in the world. The caste system there determines how rich or poor you are. In America, even though the streets are not actually paved with gold, everyone has a chance to become someone. Of course, I miss my birthplace, but when you have to survive, you do anything to achieve that goal.

Every one of us has a story to tell. Most people have moved more than once in their life. Moving is not a problem. What you do with that time is what matters. We are meant to move in this big world. We get to see so many beautiful places and enjoy God's beauty. I wouldn't trade this life for anything. I am happy. I *chose* to be happy. I *chose* to stay positive. I *chose* to live a life that makes me proud. If I had focused on my traumas, I wouldn't be where I am today. We all go through hard times in life, but I chose to conquer it all with happiness.

You live once; make the best of it. Work through your traumas, and cry when you need to so you can heal from the inside out. When you work on yourself, you become a better person for yourself *and* your family. Forgive people, and you will be much happier. I have forgiven many people who have wronged me in ways you can't imagine. Do you know who taught me to forgive? My mother, Marie. She is one tough lady and one of the wisest women I have ever met.

I leave you with this:

No matter what you choose in life, remember the little human being you once were. Would that sweet child be proud of who you have become?

God bless,

Just a girl from an orphanage, Kripa

"If I focused on my traumas, I wouldn't be where I am today. We all go through hard times in life, but I chose to conquer it all with happiness."

Kripa Reese was adopted by a loving family 21 years ago. She and her husband have eight children and homestead on a fourteen-acre farm. Kripa has been a stay-at-home mom for the last 12 years, and she absolutely loves it. However, she prefers to be called a homemaker because it sounds fancier. She loves to take her kids into the woods and go foraging and teach them all about nature, animals, and, most importantly, God. Kripa loves to tell her children about how she moved to America and never forgets all the stories about Nepal. She makes sure her children know about their Nepali heritage. She is never shy to discuss with her kids about forgiving others, treating people with kindness, and always saying hi and making conversations when meeting someone new. When she is not busy raising kids, she plays with her house plants, organizes her home, and declutters. She loves to help people because she believes this world would be a better place if every human being on earth helped each other. When you visit her, you never leave empty-handed because it is a Nepali tradition to send gifts with departing friends.

TAKING A CHANCE FOR LOVE

I had a choice to make which would change the entire trajectory of my life. I could take a risk and follow my heart towards an insane adventure or sit back and stay comfortable. I felt my life was satisfactory, but was I truly happy, personally or professionally? Anyone who knows me knows I am not one to take the easy road, but if I took this chance, it would be the most significant risk I'd ever taken.

I never anticipated the place I worked for would have such a grim future, and I never expected to fall in love with a man who lived halfway across the country. But life's beauty is that everything changes just when you think you have it all figured out. I reached a point in life where I felt love was not going to be in the cards for me until one night, out of nowhere, I met this man who made me laugh and didn't want to run for the hills after getting to know me at my core. I had built up so many walls that I felt incapable of being vulnerable in any capacity, but this man made me want to open up and give this a shot. The more we talked and got to know each other, the deeper I fell in love with him, and the physical distance between us became harder and harder to manage. They say when you know, you know, and that never really made sense to me until I met Mark. I wanted to be with him, and I knew the only way to make that happen was to leave my home and everything I had ever known.

What if it didn't work out? What if I was wrong about what we had and didn't find out until I had already moved? What if one of us changed our mind? But then again, what if it *did* work out? And what if this new adventure was exactly where and with whom I was meant to be? The prospect of this being everything I hoped it would be was worth all the risk. These thoughts constantly bounced around in my head, as this wasn't a decision I took lightly. Sometimes I tend to be too rational for my own good, and this was not only risking my heart but also stepping out of my comfort zone to follow it.

Deep down, I knew I needed to move forward and take a chance on this relationship and a new career path. Moving would never be in the cards if I couldn't find a good job where I would feel fulfilled, so I officially narrowed my job search down to the Chicago area. Several interviews later, I accepted a position with a great company and was looking forward to working with them. So it was onto the next item; where to live. Have you ever tried to buy a house in the middle of a pandemic when real estate is listed and sold quicker than you could even finish scrolling the pictures? It was not a fun time. Most of the houses we saw online were already off the market before our agent could arrange a showing. It was exhausting. It began to feel like it was never going to happen. Every declined offer felt like a blow to the gut. I cope with stress by working out, so I found myself having longer and more demanding workouts to sweat my anxiety away and coax my sanity back into existence. In the evenings, my cat and I would have dance parties, and I'm glad no one could see me while she watched me like I was insane. Instead of sleeping, I would scroll Instagram and Youtube, looking for something to distract my mind while I constantly calculated how tired I would be the next day.

Finally, one day we were touring a house, with me on a video call from my apartment in West Virginia, and Mark there in person showing me around as best he could. We found our home - this was it! I was officially moving to Chicago. My brain immediately went into go-mode and sprang into action with all the things that needed to get done: the packing (Ugh! The packing!), the paperwork, and wrapping up my life as I knew it. When the reality sank in, I began to feel extreme guilt over leaving my family and a sadness that is difficult to describe about leaving the place where I grew into who I am now. Locations become a large part of who we are. The longer we stay, the more impact they have on us. Leaving the place I'd always known was more challenging than I expected, but in all the excitement of looking forward to the next chapter, I didn't realize just how hard it would be.

Waiting for the right house to come around was almost like I was tossing an ignitor down into the pit and waiting to see if it caught fire, and the second it did, everything moved quickly. As my apartment began to fill with moving boxes and look more like a mini-warehouse than a cozy little home, I also began to feel guilty about what I was about to put my cat through, which added to the guilt I felt leaving my family. My apartment was the only home my cat had ever known, and now she would have to ride in the car for nine hours to a place where she would be afraid of both the new space and her new family. Guilt was an emotion that weighed heavily on me during this time. Was I being selfish by leaving? It's funny how it seems selfish to leave your family but altruistic to sacrifice everything for love. When you're faced with a once-in-a-lifetime opportunity, the universe tries to scare you into saying "No" so that when you say "Yes," you say it boldly and confidently, knowing deep down it is the right path for you.

My family threw a little going-away party, and later the same night, I packed what I could fit in my car, including my cat and her new car playpen, and we were on our way. I had to be in Chicago by 9:00 a.m. to sign all the documents on the house, so I left home at 11:00 p.m., teary-eyed and driving all night to make it there by morning. It was a very long night, but by the end, Mark and I were finally together, and both kitties were hiding in their new (and scary from their point of view) house!

After about a week of living in a mostly empty house, we took an Amtrak train back to pack up the rest of my things and bring them back in a moving truck. Upon arriving at the store where we rented the moving truck, they informed us they only had a much larger one available despite my advanced reservation. The truck could not fit down my one-car-wide-gravel driveway, so we loaded up my dad's pickup truck and drove it up the road to where we had parked the moving truck, essentially moving every box and piece of furniture *twice*. After a very long and hot day of double moving, I hugged my parents, and Mark and I climbed into the truck to begin our journey - home. That was the moment when it sank in for me that this was the last time I would call this place, this state, and these beautiful tree-covered hills *home*.

I began to tear up as I buckled my seatbelt. It wasn't because I was unsure of my decision but because closing one chapter, no matter how excited you are for the next, is an emotional experience. The guilt of what and who I was leaving behind flooded in - *life as I knew it changed forever*. It was not a bad thing - it was time to explore this wonderful new phase. I looked over at Mark, who could literally feel all the emotions I was exuding, and I smiled through my tears, knowing that I was making this sacrifice for our relationship and new life together.

He turned on the truck, and we headed to Chicago.

Moving anywhere comes with an adjustment of setting up a new space and getting familiar with the new surroundings, but this was on a whole new level from any moving I had experienced before. My previous moves were in areas a few hours apart, in Pennsylvania and West Virginia. It might sound crazy, but moving from such a remote area to a big city comes with some culture shock. I felt like a small, confused fish who had transferred from a large home aquarium to a freshwater lake. Everything was different; the roads, the pace, the stores, the brands, and even the temperament of the people I came across. One of the most challenging things for me at first was grocery shopping. I walked into the grocery store and felt completely overwhelmed with unknown food brands and aisles I didn't know how to navigate. I rarely left the house by myself. Every trip felt overwhelming, especially the ones I took on my own.

I am certain that simultaneously moving and starting a new career is a recipe for unsettled insanity. In this scenario, two major parts of my life were disrupted at the same time. I went from being at the top of my game in my career to learning how to navigate a new role and a new team. Then, when I finished my workday, I had more work to do as I tried to make a new place home. It was a lot of "new" and a lot of stress navigating both beginnings at once. I couldn't walk away from a mentally draining day at work and sink into the comfort of my home because it was not yet settled and homey. But like they say, home is a state of mind, and I tried my best to channel that because my heart was now home with Mark, which created a sense of peace amid the chaos. No matter what happened from this point forward, we would face it together – good and bad. I was *home*.

Moving comes with a lot of incredible new experiences too. It was so much fun setting up and decorating the new house. Making the house our own was the first step to feeling at home. I leaned into all of the projects and personalization that come with a new space, and before I knew it, I was painting doors, ripping out bushes, and putting holes in the walls to hang up art and décor that made us happy. I found just the right spot for all of my stars, pictures of people we love, art pieces I had collected over the years, and some new things we chose together. Creating and designing our space was the best part about finally owning a home. Taking an empty house and envisioning all the things I could add, remove, improve, or change was an exciting process. It gave me an outlet for creativity that I never knew I needed.

Mark and I also had a lot of fun exploring the restaurants I had never heard of and going to places I never knew existed. We have been on so many adventures since I moved here, and we have no intention of letting the adventures stop. Finding my person and taking the steps I needed to take to make our life together possible is something I will be forever grateful I took a chance on. Whether we are on a plane headed somewhere extraordinary or just relaxing at home, life is always better together.

No matter the reason for your move, be it for love, a career, a family, or a better life, it can be an overwhelming process. Especially if the place you're headed was not in your plans. I can't say that the younger version of me would have believed I'd end up here, but I did. The important thing is that you can find the feeling of *home* wherever you are. You are the most significant part of the equation. We like home because it is a part of who we are, and a move is an opportunity for you to bring that into a new space.

Bring your character, charm, and personality to your new town. Moving to a new place is an opportunity for you to expand.

You might be physically relocating, but you don't have to let go of the people you care about or the past experiences that have made you who you are. You take those people with you in your soul and in many texts and phone calls! All of the ways you've grown in your last home come with you as you make your presence known in your new space. I cycled through a myriad of emotions during this whole experience: excitement, stress, guilt, hope, sadness, and joy. Sometimes they came in groups, and sometimes one would linger longer than others, but what kept me focused on the excitement and joy was remembering why I was doing this and what it would add to my life. In the end, that was my motivation to keep moving forward.

During the chaos, I gained the opportunity to grow my relationship which ultimately led us to marriage and life together forever. Whether you moved on your own or had your family by your side, relocating takes a lot of courage. It isn't easy to step out of everything you know and start over. But there is beauty in creating new memories and going on new adventures that can lead you to places you never imagined.

"What kept me focused on the excitement and joy was remembering why I was doing this and what it would add to my life. In the end, that was my motivation to keep moving forward."

Hailey is a wife, cat mom, running enthusiast, and a full-time employee in the science and pharmaceutical industry. While she tends to be a "jack of all trades," this is her first professional writing experience. Hailey is not afraid of new challenges, evidenced in her half-cross-country move from West Virginia to Chicago. She works hard to achieve big goals and is always out to learn new things. Becoming a first-time homeowner in a huge new city gave her many learning opportunities. Life has not always been easy for

Hailey, but she has learned to set her sights high and never stop achieving the goals she sets for herself.

A HOME FOUND WITHIN

It was the hardest thing I had ever experienced, but it might not have hurt as deeply if I had known how it would end.

My fiancé, Donnie, had come home for the weekend after working in North Dakota for two weeks, and I could feel something was different. His heart wasn't in our relationship anymore, and I asked him if he wanted me to stay or leave.

He gave no answer to my question. He broke down, and we sat on the bedroom floor together and cried. It felt like a goodbye, but I didn't leave. For the next three months, if I was not at work, I lay in bed emotionally numb, staring at the wall. I felt like there was nothing else to live for and was completely empty.

We had met when I was seventeen; I was a junior, and he was a senior. I was on my high school dance team and attended the state championship tournament in the twin cities. His high school dance team also competed in the tournament, and Donnie was there with friends supporting them. We stayed at the same hotel, and he gave me his phone number before the weekend was over.

We dated long-distance until school ended for the year, and then he moved to my hometown until I graduated.

From then on, I could not imagine life without him. He was my only future, and I never created a backup plan. I was sheltered growing up in my one-stoplight town surrounded by farmland. I grew so much when I moved with my high school sweetheart, six hours away from home, where he was from, to attend college. The new area, school, and people became part of the new me. I grew into an adult there and became known by the title "Donnie's Jen."

I waited, watching that blank, empty wall from my bed during those three months hoping that something might change. I hoped that maybe, just maybe, I was dreaming and would wake up or that Donnie would suddenly beg me to stay, saying that he couldn't live without me and didn't want me to go. Around Christmas, I realized that would not happen and had no choice but to have my parents come up with a truck and trailer to get me.

We had dated for six years and were engaged for three. I was twenty-six years old and moving back home with my parents. I felt like a failure; I was embarrassed and confused. I was crushed, ripped apart, and I learned that a heart could actually ache. Such intense sadness came over me and hit me like waves. I didn't just lose a relationship. I lost the place I had created as a home, his family that I loved, and many friends (because they were his friends first). I also lost a job, over half of everything I helped work for, and the future I had planned - which was the biggest thing I couldn't wrap my head around. We were supposed to live a wonderful life and had told each other we would be in rocking chairs next to each other when we were old. The best that was yet to come wasn't coming anymore. I had lost myself and my future. I didn't know who I was or where I was going. I wasn't even sure if there was anything more to life.

I got home and unpacked my things in my old bedroom, but beyond that, I was still pretty paralyzed. I was only home two weeks before I was recruited for a job at a local bank in town. I filled the rest of my time bartending at the Moose Lodge across the parking lot from the bank. After a while, the embarrassment of returning to a place I never planned on returning to turned into acceptance. In my pursuit of distraction, the new environment caught my attention more than my loss. I pressed into work and said "Yes" to every task or extra work I was presented with, which included many public obligations since the bank and lodge were very active in my small community.

I thought that with enough time, I would heal and move on. The problem was that I had lost my future and didn't know how to plan for a new one. Everything was unknown. I was living in reaction mode. I became stuck on pause, waiting for someone or something else I could wrap my life around. My world was still about everyone else around me, even though it was no longer about my ex. I ignored myself. I didn't know who I was, nor did I ever think about what I wanted. I only knew that I hated my life.

I became extremely depressed. After work, I would come home, go to my room, and lay in bed with no sounds and little light, just staring at nothing. I felt trapped. Every day was the same thing over and over on repeat. None of my life was anything that I had chosen for myself. I was still living life as a reaction to my crushing breakup over a year later!

"Not until we are lost do we begin to find ourselves." - Henry David Thoreau

At the bank, I had a friend named Julie. She was older than me and had traveled and lived a full life. I loved working in the drive-up area with her, especially on Saturdays when I had her all to myself. She would share all her wonderful, adventurous life stories with me and tell me about all the places she had been. I lived through Julie's stories. They were the best escape from my reality and helped me believe there was more to my life than this mundane existence.

One evening at the beginning of July, I was trying to distract myself and came across a personality test to take. It was the 16 Personalities Test at www.16personalities.com, similar to the Myers-Briggs Type Indicator (MBTI). This test began for me a dive into the biggest rabbit hole I have ever gone down.

In less than twenty minutes, I discovered I was an INFP personality type. As I read my description, I felt this test understood me better than my ex did - better even than I knew myself! With every line I read, I was blown away by how this test understood how my mind worked. It felt good to be understood; it felt good not to feel alone. It had me looking inside myself, focusing my attention, and beginning to shift my mindset.

Researching my personality type became my first and favorite distraction. I read websites and books and watched YouTube videos. I loved it all; it made me feel balanced and centered. I could be me and understand why I was the way I was. I could accept myself for how I was put together and see areas where I needed to work on myself. It was like an internal road map for who I was. There were even things I came across that I had never thought about, and I questioned if these things were true for me. I learned who I was and what made me tick. It was my first shimmer of light in the darkness.

My research continued for months. I researched the best careers for my type, how I could contribute best to the world, what fulfills INFPs in life, the best ways to grow, and more. I learned from Personality Hacker on YouTube that, for my type, the best way to grow is to experience life and explore. As I was learning who I was, I had so many pieces come together for me; a new mindset and new concepts and ideas. But I was still only living through Julie's stories. I was still lost and *waiting* for life to happen to me or for someone to take me away and give me grand adventures like Julie's.

It was October 22, 2016. I was working the drive-up in the bank with Julie. She, as always, had me captivated by a story. Finally, I thought, "WHY NOT ME?! Who says I can't go to these places and see these things? I want to have a whole life of stories with pictures on my dresser, like at the end of the Titanic movie, and I don't have to wait for anyone else to have them. I am done with the empty cycle of my life!" Right then and there, I told Julie that I would put in a notice on Monday at the bank and Moose Lodge and that I would be done at the end of the year.

I felt so alive; I had a future! By then, I knew myself well enough that I could decide what I wanted. I went home that day more excited about life than I had ever been. Every day for two months, I dreamed, planned, and prepared. My original plan was to take off for two weeks in my car and stay in hotels. Then I would come back and find a new job, but that plan quickly changed because it felt like I would return to yet another unhappy cycle. As the ideas kept rolling in, my adventure grew into a six-month experience in a fully sustainable, converted cargo van.

With the new year of 2017, I started my new adventure and headed south in my little cargo van. I had never felt more free or alive; I was in control of my life and my future. Unlike many of my previous choices, this was finally something *I had chosen for myself.* I learned how to be true to myself and follow my heart. I felt as if I was dancing in the clouds. It was a feeling of complete alignment within myself, and I felt like I was home.

I didn't know that home was what I had found at first. It was a very odd "home" because it was not a physical home at all; I had even left my physical house. I discovered that home is a feeling, not a place. Knowing who you are makes you feel like you are at home within yourself. Home is knowing who you are, your beliefs, the foundation you stand on, your values, and what you believe in, and then being authentic to it all.

Home is in the heart; to find it, we must be true to ourselves. We must listen to ourselves and search. It is a journey and adventure all on its own. To truly know what lies within you, sometimes you must leave everything familiar behind, as I did. Your life and everything around you may change, but you will always be home if you know who you are.

"In her heart and soul, she set fire to all things that held her back, and from the ashes, she stepped into who she always was" - Atticus, The Truth About Magic

I have been traveling on the road for most of the last six years and following my heart. I have been all over the country, and the only times I have felt homesick are when I have lost myself or am unsure of who I am. At times, I have lost my comfort and confidence, but all I have to do is reassure myself of who I know I am. I read or watch videos about my personality type, which reminds me of who I am and helps me. If you hold true to who you are, you will always be home within yourself.

There is so much growth that comes from learning who you are. When everything in your life lines up with who you are, it will bring you happiness. As you discover who you are, you can better assess situations and make decisions, learn your strengths and how to build your weaknesses, and choose a career that fulfills your purpose. You will be able to teach your partner your love language so they can express love in a way you comprehend and feel, and you can learn how the important people in your life want to be loved in return. It opens up a better functioning way of life. You can also discover how you learn best. It puts you better in control of your life and future and helps you show up as your best self.

I started with the 16 Personalities test - it is quick, simple, and free. The Myers-Briggs Type Indicator (MBTI) is similar but much more in-depth. Some other options include "The Five Love Languages" by Dr. Gary Chapman, the Enneagram with nine types, the Clifton StrengthsFinder assessment that reveals your top five themes of talent, the True Colours test, and more. The Personality Hacker website has a wealth of knowledge on the Myers-Briggs and Enneagram types. They have some of my favorite videos on YouTube as well. You can also find a list of all major personality tests with links to each at https://www.workstyle.io/best-person ality-test.

My story of finding home is one of learning, growing, under-standing myself and my true authentic identity, and being brave enough to live by it. Grow and be brave, my friends!

"Your life and everything around you may change, but you will always be home if you know who you are."

Jen Veerkamp has been traveling the country and living out of her small, converted cargo van since 2017. She is an open book, a kind soul, an adventurer, a bucket list enthusiast and a guide for people who want the freedom that van life offers. She meanders and explores new areas with her sixteen-year-old chihuahua named Harley. Jen's home base is in Minnesota where she grew up, but loving anything outdoors, she feels most at home in nature. She runs a FaceBook group, "From Trapped in the Daily to Freedom," where she helps others transition into van life, freedom, and adventure and answers any questions they have along the way. If you are feeling stuck and trapped, that is the group for you. It's a place to learn all about van life and creating your own adventures! So come with your questions and stay for the community!

STARTING OVER

I was twenty-three and heartbroken. I felt like life was pressing me down, and I wanted to escape it. I knew that I needed a change, and rather than wait for it to happen naturally, I was going to force it.

I had recently failed in two relationships and dropped out of college. I felt like I was buried in a six-foot grave, and my whole life was staring down at me. I was devastated. At that point in my life, the only way I dealt with failure was to launch myself into something new. I didn't want to give myself time to heal. I wanted the situation fixed and sewed up with a lovely little ribbon. So naturally, the first thing I did to fix two failed relationships was to jump right into another one.

I didn't realize at first that it would involve flying across the USA in an airplane with nothing but a suitcase. I left my home behind, but it didn't feel like it *was* my home at the time. I was depressed and couldn't see what was happening; I didn't *want* to see what was happening. I wanted an escape - to leave and never return. So that's what I did, or I thought that's what I was doing.

Dean was an ex-boyfriend from high school, and I joked about moving to Texas with him. He was enlisted in the military with the United States Airforce. I was excited about leaving behind my failures and shortcomings, and I thought, "What the hell? It can't be any worse than what I'm dealing with here." So, I packed a suitcase against my mother's wishes and booked a one-way flight to Texas. I didn't have anything planned out, and I had no money or contacts except for Dean. He didn't know it, but he would be my savior. At least, that was my plan. I thought people always did this - they took chances and risks and ended up being completely happy. I had nothing to lose; what could go wrong?

I was nervous, but I was more scared of being on a plane for the first time than moving to a new place. Dean met me at the airport in San Antonio so early in the morning that it was still dark. I was warm from the dry air, and a quiet breeze floated through the airport parking lot. Dean had a black mustang, and as we drove down the highway, I sat back in those black leather seats looking out the window. I rolled down the window and put my hands in the silky smooth air. It was a clear moonlit night, and stars were shining in all their glory. I began to move my hand up and down as the silhouettes of the hills rolled by us. The sunrise that morning was beautiful! It was full of colorful reds, oranges, yellows, and splashes of purple that reflected off the clouds.

Because this major life change was a spur-of-the-moment decision, I didn't have a job or vehicle. I had no money, and Dean was paying for everything. So, I went job hunting! I didn't see one in the newspapers that I would qualify for, and there was nothing online, so I applied for my Certified Nursing Assistant license to be transferred to my new home. I didn't want to continue as a CNA because the job paid very little, but I didn't know what else to do.

Transferring my CNA license took several weeks, and I enjoyed my time off. I smoked outside on the patio, soaked in the warm summer sun, slept until noon, and relaxed. Eventually, my CNA certification came through, and I had to start working again. At that point, most of my life changes had treated me well!

Everything was turning out well except for our relationship. I craved intimacy, and Dean wasn't the type of man who loved openly. Intimacy was difficult for him because of his past trauma. He had been overseas on active duty in the military, where he had been a part of some serious events. Seeing and experiencing violent acts can leave our souls tired and worn. Maybe that's why I felt there was a distance between us that we could not close.

I also didn't give myself time to heal from my past relationships and wasn't ready to be with someone new. I was trying to run from the heartache of the past and wanted to be held and loved for the unique person that I was, but I wasn't ready to give that love to someone else. I knew Dean felt like he loved me, but he didn't show me affection, and I felt unloved. I began withdrawing from Dean when he didn't love me in the way I needed, and he sensed I was drifting away.

Dean had three roommates when I first moved in, but during that year, they all moved out for love or military reasons. I had a low-paying job, and Dean was not a high-level military man with a lot of funds. We decided to move into a cheaper rental in the shady part of town, but we still needed more money to pay our bills. We couldn't live on base because Dean and I were not married, so we got a roommate.

Dean was a recovering alcoholic and had been maintaining his sobriety fairly well. He was a great person who was battling PTSD, and in the past, he had self-medicated with alcohol which only made things worse. Dean really missed drinking because that was a big part of his social life. Most military personnel liked to drink, and they drank *a lot*. He was left out of all the E-Club invites, house parties, and holidays when he didn't drink.

He started drinking again while we were visiting one of my friends from Michigan. I discovered that Dean was entirely different when he was drunk - his entire demeanor changed. He may not have been intimate with me when sober, but he was respectful. When drunk, Dean was rude and insulting. He wanted to know why I hadn't done the laundry or the dishes and would drag me over to the spots of uncleanliness and point to them. Apparently, it was *my* job to make sure they got done. The conclusion I drew from his behavior was that he was hurting and didn't want to hurt alone.

The drinking continued. At first, it was just once and a while, but soon we had beer in the fridge all the time. One night, he got really drunk and started staring me down as if I was hiding something. He got two inches from my face and started yelling at me. I felt uncomfortable and belittled, but he was looking for a fight. I don't remember what words were thrown around, but I slapped him. I felt humiliated! To lose control of myself and slap someone else was wrong on every level, but he wouldn't back off.

I kept trying to achieve his affection, but Dean never saw *me*. I could have gone into outer space and retrieved a star that would burn with an eternal flame, and he wouldn't have appreciated it. He *certainly* didn't appreciate me. His drinking got worse, and one night things got so rough in the bedroom that I felt scared. Another night he went out with his friends at the e-club and became black-out-drunk. I picked him up, and as we drove a few miles away from the E-Club, he started to relive his past traumas. He seemed to calm down while I was driving, so I continued to drive for hours, hoping he would sober up a little bit to avoid problems.

As time went on, things got worse between us. One of my friends saw the signs of abuse and warned me to get out of the relationship *fast*. At that time, I didn't understand what she was referring to, I was so numb and naive, but I soon found out.

We had several fights where he got just inches from my face and stared me down, but I never slapped him again. He made accusations and told me that I had *nowhere* to go and *nobody was there for me*. During another argument, I put my hand on his chest to lightly push him off me and out of my face, which only upset him. He screamed, "Don't you push me," and started to back me into a wall. I cried, "Why don't you just hit me," baiting him. I knew that if he hit me, I would have reason to leave him. I felt so low that I didn't care anymore if he hit me. I backed up against the wall, and he punched clean through the sheetrock inches from my head. I don't know if he missed or chose to punch the wall instead of my head, but I shut up after that. I found out that being yelled at might not be as bad as being hit.

When he sobered up the next day, he was mad at himself. He looked at the hole in the wall and told me it could have been my head. I informed him that I would leave if anything remotely related to that event ever happened again. I also told him that if his friends wanted to go out drinking, they could deal with him. At that point, I didn't care if he was out with other women, men, or ducks - I didn't want to deal with him when he was drunk.

After that, his drinking slowed down for a while, and I thought we would make the relationship work. I decided to return to college because more education would allow me to obtain a higher-paying job. I enrolled and got accepted into the University of Texas, a challenging hour-and-a-half drive from where we lived.

The distance meant I would be there for hours because I couldn't leave the school between classes to go home. I spent so much time there that he accused me of cheating on him (as if I had time for that).

He eventually went out drinking again, and one night, I picked him up drunk. He wasn't blacked out, but he was close. As we were entering our house, he turned quickly back toward me for some unknown reason, and I flinched, which made him angry. At first, I thought he was mad at himself for causing me to flinch, but that wasn't the case. I tried to walk away, but that made him angrier. He was getting close to me again but seemed to come to his senses and ran out the front door.

He called his superiors and asked them to come to the house to ensure everything was okay because he feared what he would do to me. I said that I was "fine," but I wasn't. I was afraid of what his superiors would do if I told the truth. Where would I go? What would happen to Dean? I didn't want anything to happen to him on my account. His superiors talked with him for a while and eventually left in the morning. I was done after that, done with the fighting, the emotional abuse, and the toxic relationship between us both.

I got the college to agree to let me finish the semester virtually. I talked to all my professors and the college counselor and jumped through a ton of hoops just to leave a man who was, at the very least, emotionally abusive to me. My counselor told me some stories of women physically forced to stay and told me to pack in secret. I quit my job and quietly started packing. I planned to put whatever I could carry into my car, including my dog and myself, and drive back to Michigan to live with my parents. I was afraid of Dean, but he was mad and not talking to me then. I don't think he knew I was packing or planning my exit until five days before my departure.

The last few days, my packing became obvious, and I felt he had a right to know that I was leaving, so I told him. He thought we were just taking a break from our relationship as I had been sleeping on the couch while he was on the bed. He said we should have some time to breathe before making up our minds. He didn't know I had been planning this for months with my school and counselors. I ended our relationship in a state of complete numbness - I didn't cry or yell. I was exhausted from college classes, homework, and life.

I filled the car with as much as it could carry and left, driving twenty-three hours from Texas to Michigan. I may have started my journey brokenhearted, but I was much worse when I returned home. I didn't feel anything - I was numb and dead inside. I viewed love as dead and concluded that it didn't exist.

My family opened their arms to me when I came back home. They loved me enough to take me back into their home. They believed they should be there for family and do whatever it took to get them back on their feet. Their love made my transition back from the darkness of my mind possible. I felt overwhelming gratitude and safety once I moved back. I was so thankful I had a place to go; it was home.

There is always a chance to start over a second time, a third time, a fourth time, a fifth time, or *as many times as you need*. There are outlets if you are in an unsafe environment within your home for any reason. There are places to go, and I urge you to leave before things get abusive toward yourself or others. You can go home to your family, stay at your friend's house, go to a shelter for battered women, or move out on your own.

There are many reasons to leave a relationship; you don't need a perfect reason. Emotional or physical abuse is not worth it: *leave*. You are not an inconvenience to those who you go to for help. People who love you would rather help you than find that you died either by someone else's hands or your own. The grief they would feel at your loss would create a chasm that could never be filled. *You deserve better*; the beauty is that you *always* have a chance to start over.

About the Author

"I packed a suitcase against my mother's wishes and booked a one-way flight to Texas."

Ella Marie is an adventurer. She loves to be spontaneous and loves all outdoor adventures. Traveling, sightseeing, and rock climbing are her favorite outdoor activities. Sunshine is Ella's antidote for hard days, and even on hard days, Ella continuously looks for the best outcomes. Ella's words of encouragement to women are, "You don't need a man to save you from everything you have gone through. You can do that yourself. You have everything you need to turn your life around and start to live a life you love."

DREAMING BIG, GOING SMALL

I have moved 21 times in my life, but none of those moves compare to this one.

I started thinking about the world differently when I was pregnant with my first child and began learning how to live in a more healthy way and give my child the best possible life. My husband and I were pushing toward a life that *we thought* would be perfect. We had a large house with all the things; we were in a nice neighborhood with manicured lawns and a cute little park for the kids to play "safely" with fake turf ground. We had a beautiful community with friendly neighbors and plenty of sidewalk space for our nightly stroller walks. But, as my husband and I grew into our parenthood more and more, we realized we wanted our children immersed in nature. Not only to go on our weekly state park trips that we all looked forward to so much but actually to *live* on some land with our *own* hiking trails. That wasn't going to happen in our neighborhood with "turf" grass and sidewalks. We were ready for a change.

Both my husband and I *knew* we needed to make a change and move to a place that would offer adventure and awakening. We had no clue *where*, but we knew we wanted to live somewhere where we could have the forest just a few steps from our door. We wanted a place where we could live off the land, raising our children to learn how to care for themselves and, someday, their own families. We desired to go back to a simple and wholesome lifestyle and teach our children the real meaning of life.

We started staying up late and watching YouTube videos of people that had moved to the woods. They didn't have running water, and they didn't have conventional heat - they just used their woodstoves. It was like these people took a trip back into a time when life was simple, hard work was everything, and we learned everything we needed to know from nature and God's green Earth. As we watched, we thought, "We could totally do that - leave right now and live in a small place, as long as we had the land to live on and the love in our hearts!" Little did I know that watching those videos every night and dreaming of the possibilities would start a fire within us that would continue to grow.

We started looking for houses, but the timing wasn't right. I quit my job as a full-time educator soon after our second child joined our family. All that time, we kept looking and didn't find *anything* that seemed right. A couple of years passed, and our third child was almost ready to join our family. Just a few months before he was born, my husband, Eric, got offered a new job about an hour and a half away. This job was completely unplanned and would be something a good friend of mine would call a "God wink" because it landed him in a spot that would be the catalyst to finding our dream home.

Our moving journey started in 2020 when the big "housing market" craze began. We didn't know how selling our home would even go due to the worldly events happening because of covid. We did, however, see the effects when it came to searching for a home to buy. Every time we thought we would find a house we wanted to look at, just a few hours would pass, and it would be marked "pending sale." It was a roller coaster of emotions to find a house we liked, and then we felt the pressure of quickly setting up a time to go to a showing just to be told it was no longer available. Finally, we found a house we liked online that we could see the next day. We were excited and anxious as we packed up our family and made the hour-and-a-half drive.

I remember the drive like it was yesterday. It seemed like it was taking forever to get there because all we saw after we got off the highway were farmer's fields and trees. It was a good 25 minutes away from any gas station or ma and pa grocery store. We were immediately in awe when we finally pulled into what was supposed to be the house's driveway. We turned onto a dirt sliver of a road that led us through the woods. It was like the woods were swallowing us up! We looked at each other with wide eyes and excitement as we continued down the path. Then, as we followed the dirt road and pines, we caught sight of the cutest little cabin in the woods. It looked like a real-life version of an "Up North Minnesota" postcard. As Eric put the van in park, before even stepping foot in the house, we looked at each other and exclaimed, "This is it!" Immediately, I had peace in my heart and complete clarity, knowing that *this* was where we were supposed to be.

After viewing our new forever forest home, I still had peace in my heart *and* a new challenge. The home we fell in love with was only 704 square feet. When we told people, they thought we were crazy to move into such a small house with three young children. They gave a very slow "are you serious" look because of the size and because it was right by the river. They didn't think that was safe for our children. And not only was it small, but it only had a lofted bedroom and an office bedroom, which according to others, was "not accommodating" for us. They often said, "How will your children have their own space?" There was no garage, no outbuilding, nothing as far as that goes. They also thought moving far away from family was not a good choice. We felt a lack of support from some people and silence from others, but we were sure of our decision. We just needed to prepare for such a drastic change of space.

Aside from the typical ups and downs with the process of buying a house, becoming minimalists was one of the biggest challenges we had to navigate. How would we (a family of five with a newborn) become minimalists and go from a 2,000 sq ft house to a 704 sq ft cabin home with ZERO closets? It *seemed* simple - we just had to get rid of practically EVERYTHING! We had about two months to prepare for this ENORMOUS change and to go through our entire life's belongings to decide what was purposeful enough to bring along. We were the typical family with crowded closets, cupboards, and garages, but the number of things we had stashed away will forever change my view on the things we *need* and the things we *choose* that bury us.

I remember getting rid of 10 extra large garbage bags of just clothes! We were dominating all the "sell-it" groups and loading them with gobs and gobs of our unwanted junk - just begging people to take it. We were selling things so quickly and to so many people that I remember finally putting all of the "sold" items outside, doing mass batches of "porch pick up," and going on the trust system of people putting the money under the doormat. I went through weeks of digging, packing, bagging, and posting to get rid of everything we could. We finally reached a point where our family shared a mattress on the floor, dug our clothes out of baskets, and ate dinner on the floor (don't worry, we had plates). We made a couch out of extra blankets and sat on the floor. We had gotten rid of what we thought was everything, and now we needed all of the buying processes to line up and be ready to move into our dream home.

It is hard to describe the challenges we went through with the journey of selling a home at the same time as buying a new one. We had "special" challenges that caused us stress during that time. There were delays because some government offices were closed due to the pandemic. There was another CASH offer on our cabin home, and we had to write a letter of intent to convince the sellers to sell to us. And we had been told we would have a delayed closing date on our current home, but at the last minute, it was kept on the original date, and we had to rush and move our things to the garage in less than 24 hours! It was a long and bumpy journey! But those aren't the details that matter.

Most importantly, my family and I had followed a path the Lord laid in our hearts and lives, and we were finally through those bumps. We did it! And we were finally on our way to our NEW home - it was such a surreal moment. Eric and I were holding the keys to the home we had dreamt about so much. The Lord had answered our prayers as we worked to manifest our dreams. It literally felt like a big pinch-me moment, and we were overcome with joy as we listened to our boys singing songs and talking about building forts in the woods, collecting pine cones, and even helping collect wood for our fires! We felt the weight on our shoulders lifted and enjoyed the long drive with gratitude. Eric dropped the kids and me off with a small load, then drove back to our old garage and picked up another load of belongings. My mom, brothers, and many others immediately came to our new home to congratulate us. It was such a celebration and will forever be burned in my memory and heart.

We have lived here for two and a half years, and it has already brought so much peace and gratitude to our hearts to live in such a tranquil cabin home. There are definitely challenges living in such a small space. My husband is tired of me changing the furniture in all of the rooms in hopes that it will help our small space get more organized and be more functional, but we are still working on minimizing and trying to live with fewer things. It takes time and patience to perfect and master significant change, but let me tell you all that we have gained! We have boys who seek peace, imagination, gratitude, and strength in the woods, and we have land in place of things that help our dreams grow each day. And oh, the memories we have made in that peaceful river already - I can't imagine our world without it! We have a tiny cabin to help us stay close to each other, and we have countless memories of picking berries, hunting wildlife, raising animals, and so much more!

When moving, you need to be fluid and flexible. If you are rigid, it will hurt, and you'll break. Go with the flow of things; if you don't, it makes everything harder. Shift your mindset to *believe* that things will work out how you want them to, even when you can't see them. Our hard work and all our late nights manifesting our dream life came to fruition, and our prayers were answered! Moving to our dream property allowed us to establish our desired life - giving back and becoming a good wholesome, closely connected, nature-immersed family.

If you find yourself navigating all that comes with a move, stay in the moment. It can be tempting to wish the process away, but you are in the moment you're supposed to live right now. Take a deep breath and focus on the next step, one breath at a time.

ABOUT THE AUTHOR

"It can be tempting to wish the process away, but you are in the moment you're supposed to live right now. Take a deep breath and focus on the next step, one breath at a time."

Kirsten is a fierce and passionate mom, educator, and nature enthusiast. Her family finds peace when deeply immersed in nature. She founded Organic Roots School in 2021, a micro-school that focuses on a combination of Forest School Montessori and Waldorf education. Teaching children through nature is Kirsten's purpose in this world. Kirsten teaches academics with a strong focus on helping her students become amazing humans. She teaches her students that they can be passionate about *anything*, not just reading and math, and how creativity, play, and imagination are powerful. Kirsten teaches her students that they can do anything they put their minds to, and their shine never fades.

THE TINY TOWN

I had moved many times in my life due to being a military kid, but as I approached high school, I started to build roots for the first time. After all, my dad was retiring from the military, so we had no need to move again, right? Boy, was I wrong. I was in for the surprise of my life, but not in a good way. Despite all my prior moves, this one was different.

I got comfortable after the final military move before my dad's retirement when I turned thirteen. I had overcome the misery that was middle school and spent my first two years of high school building the life I wanted, and it was going great.

I was involved in all the school activities, so I would have my pick of college to attend. Because of this, I connected with lots of people, which helped build my friend circle. I was even actively involved in my passion, horse riding. I was having lots of fun in club meetings, hanging out with friends, and enjoying life. The only thing I could complain about was that the guys I liked didn't like me back. But, if that was the worst thing happening, it wasn't all that bad (even if it felt like a soul-sucking disaster at the time).

As I approached the end of my sophomore year of high school, I was even more excited when my parents discussed their plans for after his retirement. They told me Dad would get a job locally, and we would not have to move. I rejoiced, celebrated, and told all my friends I wasn't going anywhere with a giddy, excited attitude and a grin from ear to ear. I thought of all the possibilities the next year would hold, such as running for class officer, continuing to spend time in my clubs and activities, and becoming an even better rider.

Everything was going great until my bubble popped. My parents told us my dad had secured a job for when he reached his retirement with the Navy. He would be working for the power company that provided electricity to most parts of the state. However, the location they needed him to go and work would be on the other side of the state, the part that bordered West Virginia.

At first, I shrugged it off. While I was looking forward to my dad not being gone all the time and missing things due to his deployments and overnight duty schedules, his coming home every weekend to spend with us would be ok. Nope. That wasn't the plan. We were *all* going.

I was crushed and devastated. My plans for the next year and, frankly, the rest of my life went up in smoke. Didn't they tell me we were staying? Didn't they care that I had built my life to right where I thought it should be, and it would all come crashing down? In my small group at church that week, I told them what was happening through teary eyes and sobs. I cried on the neck of my favorite horse during my next riding lesson and treasured every minute with her.

After that, I hit denial. I wasn't going. Through gritted teeth, I made up my mind. I was going to find a way. I was convinced that God would not let this happen to me. Not after all the moves I had been through and how great my life had finally become. When my dad asked if I wanted to go with them for the weekend to the town we would be moving to, I said, "No." I had no intention of going to a place I had decided *I* would not be moving.

Unfortunately, I was still a minor, and although he asked, he would not let me stay behind. I had to go on the house hunting trip. My parents were excited about a house they had identified when they were there before. That is where we spent most of our time. After looking around the ancient house, I found a room away from the rest of my family, crouched down, and cried. Being there squashed my bubble of denial; it was really happening. My brother and sister, seemingly unphased by all of this, happened to come into the room and see me. They rolled their eyes, laughed, and told me to get over it.

When we got back, I continued with my summer, still telling myself I would do whatever I had to not to go, although I didn't believe it as much anymore. While my family packed up the rest of the house, I left my things as they were. The week before we were to move, I went to spend a week in New Orleans with my grandparents, which we had done in the summer numerous times before. After I got back, I attended a lock-in at a church with a friend. We stayed up all night, and things were as I thought they should be until the next day.

My parents had packed up my stuff and moved while I was at my grandparent's house, and my dad came to get me after the lock-in to bring me to my new home. When he picked me up, I stared out the car window with tears streaming down my face until I fell asleep. Thankfully, I had been up all night and passed out quickly and easily. How awkward the trip would have been otherwise since I replaced my denial with disdain for my dad. I decided that Dad, who I felt was responsible for the whole thing, was no longer worth being a part of my life. Since he didn't seem to care about my trauma, I would pretend he wasn't there. This attitude lasted into my senior year of high school.

I lay in bed each night for the next three months and cried before falling asleep. I often thought about taking off in the car to go home, and I lost all interest in anything I would have previously found important or exciting. I moped my way through each day. My mom felt sad for me, but neither of my parents offered anything of value to help.

The school didn't help the situation. People there were very different from those I had built relationships with in my old school. I didn't get involved in any activities. The town we moved to had less than ten traffic lights. It took twenty minutes on the interstate to get to the next town with the Walmart, movie theater, and McDonald's. The town's population was only about double that of the high school I had attended before. I couldn't find anywhere to continue riding and missed horse time terribly. I kept to myself and didn't make friends until much later on.

We started attending the church down the street, and I began to connect with the youth pastor there. He and his wife were good people and seemed to care about how down I was, which was a different feeling from what I was getting at home. One night after the youth group, I sat and talked with them alone. During our discussion, we determined having a job might help as it would give me something constructive to do, and I could earn some money to pay for the gas to visit the closest large city an hour away. We prayed, and I started to feel better.

The youth pastor's wife worked at a camp about 30 minutes away. She put in a word for me with the manager over the camp store and snack bar. I went out to meet with him and discuss the possible job opportunity. The camp was amazing. I had never heard of YoungLife before, but the beauty and atmosphere of the place were breathtaking. It was evident God's presence was there, and I had never experienced anything like that before. I felt at peace and relieved for the first time in months.

I ended up getting the job, which was great. I also met the local leader of the YoungLife group and connected with her. She invited me to join their weekly meetings, so I did. Things started to get less gloomy from there. I met a girl in the YoungLife group who became my best friend - the best friend I had ever had before. I enjoyed my job, was good at it, and met many people. The campers, who were my age, came from different places each weekend. I also became a camper and volunteered at other YoungLife camps over the summer.

My relationship with God grew to a level I had never experienced before. I started reading my Bible, memorizing verses, and regularly hanging out with the YoungLife group, leading to worshiping more often. While I still hung onto things from home and didn't put down any roots or get as deeply involved as I had previously been, I had gotten to a place of being ok.

Looking back on it now, I can see how God used this move to redirect my life. I could have easily gone down a path that would have prevented me from being who He made me to be and who I am today if I had stayed in my hometown.

I have realized from my experience that recognizing mental illness and addressing it right away is essential. I was definitely depressed after the move. I grieved the loss of friends, experiences, and the school I loved and valued. I mourned the loss of the person I had become in my old city. She was gone, and that was very tough to navigate without professional guidance (which I received later in life and had great success with). Of course, God provided for me and gave me the YoungLife leader and youth pastor, but I may not have struggled so much as an adult had I been through therapy and learned valuable skills sooner. If you or a family member is depressed, seek help as soon as possible.

I have learned the importance of knowing my worth, working on myself, and regularly assessing where I am and where I want to go. Had I known my internal worth and value at the time, I may not have been so hung up on the identity I had developed in my prior home. Now that I know my real worth and value and that it's tied to God and not anyone or anything else, nothing on this earth can remove it. Know that you are a person of great worth and value, regardless of external circumstances.

I also learned to turn to God in hard times. Finding a supportive church community early on was a game-changer for me. I don't know how I could have continued in my depressed emotional state had I not gotten involved in YoungLife. Turning to God and faith organizations that support you will change your life.

Lastly, I learned that I don't know the whole story or picture, but God does, and even painful experiences can bring good. I'll never know what detrimental path might have awaited me without the intervention of the move I didn't want. But I do know that a chain of events was set in motion that led me to the wonderful husband and amazing children I have now. God met me where I was and provided what I needed to grow; I'll always be grateful for that. Let God meet you where you are. He knows what you need and will provide.

About the Author

"Know that you are a person of great worth and value, regardless of external circumstances."

Sara Garnett is a working mom of two, an avid horse lover, and a personal development enthusiast. She loves to help women live the lives they were meant to instead of letting life happen to them. She also speaks with organizations about how they can help their employees live their best lives and therefore show up as their best selves to work, their families, and the community.
Sara's dad spent 20 years in the military before retiring. She moved every 1-3 years and went to 8 different schools from kindergarten to graduation. As described in the chapter, the final move set off mental illness that she had to overcome through therapy and other tools learned as an adult. After finally stabilizing her life, she shares

her planning and organization strategies with other overwhelmed working moms. Visit her site or social media profiles to learn more!

500 MILES

5 00 miles.

It might not seem that far, but my entire family lived within a five-mile radius, and no one had ever moved anywhere outside of that area, so it felt like an eternity away.

But I needed it.

My dream was lofty: I wanted to work for Canada's Prime Minister (the equivalent of the President of the United States). I did everything possible to achieve that dream – I studied political science at university, interned for the federal government during school summers, and even volunteered on campaigns that supported our Prime Minister. I was lucky enough to be chosen to intern for the Prime Minister for one of my summer positions. It was amazing, and I knew that was what I was meant to do.

It wasn't out of necessity to be seen or heard that I wanted to work for our Prime Minister; instead, I desired to be in the thick of it, designing policy that helped everyday Canadians. I wanted to make their lives easier and help them be more fulfilled. I believed that I needed to be where the policies were being developed so that I could make a lasting impression and impact on my country and the world around me. It wasn't just a few people that I felt needed changed policies; an entire nation of hardworking Canadians needed relief from government taxes, unseen procedures, red tape, and being nickeled and dimed.

My first job out of university wasn't working directly for the Prime Minister, but it was working for a Minister of the Crown appointed by our Prime Minister, which was good enough. If the Prime Minister (PM) appointed them, then I was, in a sense, working for him! Or at least, that is how I saw it.

The only problem with this gigantic dream was that our capital city was in Ottawa, which was 500 miles away from my hometown, and I had no support system in Ottawa. I knew almost no one in the city. I relied on my support system at home because they were the people that kept me connected to my community. They kept me down-to-earth, humble, and grounded when I was too far in the clouds, and they gave me a helping hand or a listening ear when I was down.

I needed a support system because I didn't know anyone in the Ottawa community. I needed people that would encourage me when I felt down and celebrate with me when I was excited. These small acts of kindness kept me feeling emotionally healthy and complete. I was worried that if I moved so far away from my support system, I would become depressed and not know how to get out of it, but I also had a goal so big that I couldn't stay.

I wanted this so badly that I knew my introverted self needed to do this. I needed to step outside of my comfort zone and enter my new world, and boy, was it worth it.

I landed in a hostel for two weeks after my five-hundred-mile trek to Ottawa, which was terrifying. I shared a room with seven other people and didn't even have a locker to keep my stuff locked up. Luckily, I was fortunate, and nothing went missing, but the noise of seven other people sleeping meant I didn't get much sleep.

The work was wonderful, and I am thankful I immediately excelled at it, but I *still* didn't know anyone in the city when I moved into my first apartment. I was starting to feel alone and secluded even though I was surrounded by people. I didn't know what to do to rectify that, and being an introvert meant I had no idea what to do next or how to meet people outside of work. Just because one aspect of my life was fulfilling didn't mean every part was.

I'd love to say that I embraced my fears and met new people, but I didn't at first. I thought that physically leaving an abusive situation and other traumas behind would encourage me to thrive. Instead, when I no longer had my support system, everything I was running away from managed to accumulate and smack me across the face all at once. I retreated and sunk into a deep depression. Even though I got up every day and worked with a happy demeanour, that happiness took everything I had to muster up. In the evenings, I slept - sometimes from when I got home till I went back to work the next day, and weekends were the worst. Sometimes I would sleep the entire weekend away. I couldn't understand why I was unhappy because I was so fulfilled in my career and thought that was all I needed. What was I missing?

But in reality, the lack of human contact started to weigh on me and bring me further down. That spiraling continued until I was getting ready for work one day, and none of my clothes fit.

Depression made it hard to get out of bed. Scraping myself out of my apartment and into work took all my energy. I have poor genes and gain weight easily. Because I understood this, I had kept active as much as possible throughout my teen years and early 20s. But as much as I wanted to continue to be active at this point in my life, I just couldn't. This lack of exercise increased my weight almost a hundredfold, and eventually, my clothes just didn't fit. I went to work that day in the only thing I could muster on, knowing full well that I would have to get new clothes that evening and that I needed to start exercising again.

That day was the beginning of my transformation.

I realized that there was more to life than work. I needed connection with other people to be fulfilled completely.

Don't get me wrong. It took a lot of trial and error to find people I enjoyed spending time with and find things I could do to meet others. But this was where I started — finding connection was my impetus.

I searched on Facebook and Google, read local newspapers, and found community boards with events happening in my city that I could attend to meet new people. I was saddled with a fair amount of school debt, so I didn't have much money to do expensive things, but I knew that some things had to become a priority again. Creating friendships, restoring my mental and emotional health, and even just going out and meeting new people were now at the top of the list.

I went to community events, attended presentations at the Library and Archives Canada, walked through the tulips at the Tulip Festival (one of the largest events in my new town), and bought skates so I could skate on the canal in the winter. I even scrimped and saved so I could go to a new restaurant once a month and enjoy a beautiful meal. Food is important to me, so I made it a priority in my budget to enjoy the lovely, award-winning restaurants in Ottawa.

My physical health also needed to be a priority, along with my emotional health, so I found a local community gym and worked out there three times per week at least. I made it a goal to talk to one person each time I went. I didn't make many friends, but at least we recognized each other when we went to the gym and talked a bit. I was making strides.

I found other active groups that met outside from spring to fall and made a few friends. I joined a church and made a few lifelong friends. I also joined a book club at our community center and enjoyed engaging in intellectual activities.

These events and occasions changed the way I felt emotionally. Once I started opening up and engaging in my community, I began to feel more like myself and less depressed. Sometimes all you need is fresh air, community with new people, and a common goal to lift you out of that depression.

I also engaged in counseling because I needed a safe space to get over the abuse I had received for most of my life. However, I would have never felt comfortable getting counseling in the depths of my depression.

I lost a bit of weight physically and a lot of emotional baggage by increasing my social circle. I started connecting with my community and made friends outside my workplace. This connection with like-minded people helped me feel more like myself. I finally had the support I needed when the bad days came and when we celebrated the good times.

Furthermore, I realized I didn't have to be physically in the same location to remain in close contact with someone. I wrote and texted my friends back home and kept those relationships strong, too. I realized that as long as I was willing to continue to open up to someone, I could still keep the closeness I had when we were physically close. I wrote about my feelings, which was hard for me, and I talked about what I was doing to feel better connected. My friends loved that I was growing and feeling better emotionally, and they were still there to support me when times were tough. I had forgotten that when I was depressed.

Learning all of this was almost magical. I started feeling better about myself, my career, my health, and my emotions. I learnt that relationships take time and that everyone has been a new person before. This perspective gave me compassion and helped me more easily connect with others.

I did end up working for our Prime Minister and fulfilling my dreams, but the only reason I got that opportunity was that I stepped out of my comfort zone and met the Director of Tour and Scheduling (I was an Event Coordinator). If I had continued to hide and be depressed, I would not have bothered to apply to my dream job or say "Yes" to unique opportunities. I had the amazing opportunity to schedule every event the Prime Minister had for over two years (and I did half of them one year!). The only way for a new policy to be helpful to the public is if they know about it, and I had the incredible opportunity to share that information.

Because I stepped out of my comfort zone and met with the Director of Tour and Scheduling, she saw who I was and what I believed. Our ideas and priorities aligned, and she felt I would make a great addition to the team. If I was still depressed and without a support system, I am not sure I would have ever reached out and met with her; I would have felt unworthy or that I didn't belong. Stepping out of my comfort zone helped me achieve my goals, but only because I was emotionally healthy at the time.

I left Ottawa five years later for my hometown again, but just because I was heading back to my hometown didn't mean that I hadn't changed over the years. I was armed with resources and ideas for making new connections this time. Texting, emailing, and phone calls were a part of that. I also knew how to find community events through local newspapers, Facebook groups, the community center, nonprofits, and farmer's markets. I also learned to keep in contact with people instead of retreating into a depression.

I remember those in Ottawa and still keep in touch. I have learned how to meet people online and develop relationships with those I may never have the chance to meet in person. We *can* take the first step and reach out to new people to forge connections. Stepping out of our comfort zone is the only way we will meet new people and do new things.

W*e need people* to survive this crazy world. Doing everything on our own gets exhausting and unbearable. Stepping out of my comfort zone and taking the first step made me happy and content. Continuing to meet people and develop new and long-term relationships perpetuates that happiness. I know from experience that without a support system, some, like myself, sink into depression. I now make it a priority to continue building a support system, and I know that *you* can develop a support system too.

"We need people to survive this crazy world. Doing everything on our own gets exhausting and unbearable."

With a grand total of 28 moves (as of publication), Sharlene is happy to settle into a more permanent move this year. She knows of the stress of moving many times, which has helped her focus on the financial side of things to help empower more women to live financially abundant lives.

Sharlene has created a strategy that demolished her debt in 5 years on an income of less than $55K even though she wasn't legally allowed to make more income. This strategy has been crafted to help women of any financial level create lasting financial freedom.

She would love you to join her as you navigate personal and business finance.

Using Adventure to Find Home

M y family went from California to Italy the first time I ever moved, but I didn't think it was a big deal. I was only nine years old, and my parents framed it as a big adventure. I learned that a move could be fun when you treated it like an adventure and looked forward to exploring your new space. But could I implement this same attitude for my next move?

As a child, despite being unimpressed with the idea of leaving California, the actual move to Italy was a big one. Movers packed up the house, and our goods were shipped and set to arrive about a month after we did. Italy was very different from California. We had come to a new place with a new language, new food, and a new climate. My parents insisted my sister and I try new foods because the only way you can know what you like is to taste things, and we had to do that only a few days after arriving in Italy! We went to a restaurant recommended as an excellent place to find a variety of familiar food. My sister and I ordered fried shrimp.

We expected golden brown shrimp with tails attached that were crunchy and delicious. The plates set down in front of us were not what we expected. They were filled with shrimp freshly caught from the nearby ocean that were lightly battered and fried *with their heads and shells on*! I had never even thought about what shrimp looked like before! My parents patiently prepped those plates into something my sister and I could and would eat, and it was ultimately tasty enough that it wasn't the last time we ordered it before we moved again.

My parents took advantage of where we were and what was nearby, so we spent Christmas in Rome one year and went to Greece over a holiday weekend. As a kid, these short trips were not unfamiliar, but the destinations were much more fun than when we went to San Francisco or Oakland since I'd been there so much. Cobblestone streets in Rome were so fun to walk on, and the Sistine Chapel had just been restored and was gorgeous. I threw a coin over my shoulder into the Trevi Fountain, which means I will be back, according to legend. The visit to Greece required taking a ferry. One way was overnight, and we slept through the choppy water. The way back was during the day, and my sister and I played Ms. Pac-Man for hours near the deck where we could see the ocean we were crossing. I had never seen cars drive onto a boat before!

My dad's job had taken us across the world and back, and I figured it would happen again. When we moved back to California about a year and a half after our move to Italy, I started to picture my future full of living in new places. I didn't know how personally I would take the next move or when it would happen. I settled back into elementary school and weekend drives around the Bay Area.

When I was a freshman in high school, my parents sat down and explained we were moving to Japan. I was a fourteen-year-old who loved high school. I was involved in student council, had friends I loved spending time with, had plans for spring sports, and had to leave it *all* behind. I just knew my parents were doing this to me on purpose. They were intentionally ripping me away from everything I knew and loved and taking me halfway around the world to start over because they were mean. I remembered my school in Italy and knew the one in Japan would also be small. Moving in the middle of the year meant kids my age had formed their social groups, and I dreaded trying to find my way. My hopes of continuing in student council or any leadership role were dashed. My parents were as encouraging as they could be despite also stepping into the unknown, but I never once thought of their perspective.

We were given a weight restriction that limited how many rooms in the house could go with us. My parents decided not to ship a vehicle or appliances based on their experience moving to Italy. It allowed us more weight for boxes, and they could purchase a car and use the laundromat once we were in Japan. I reluctantly helped pare down my belongings to what we could pack and ship. It was an excellent chance to go through my clothes and only keep the items that fit, but choosing only some of my books was hard. Some things were easier to part with, like the cast I had worn the previous fall and toys I had long outgrown. I had two suitcases of clothes and a few other items for our initial travels and arrival in Japan; everything else was packed and shipped, sold in a garage sale, or given away.

Once we arrived in Japan, I sullenly participated in exploring the new area. It was difficult to get used to the new time zone while feeling unsettled. My parents had thoughtfully mailed small gifts to my sister and me ahead of time, so we immediately had a package to open. We spent time with several of my dad's coworkers and their families as they showed us around and shared things that helped them when they had first moved to the area. I appreciated being on a smaller campus when I started school. It was much easier to navigate my way from class to class than at my previous school. It took some time and some tears, but I realized that my life would be easier if I stopped insisting on taking a negative viewpoint on every aspect of living in Japan.

I appreciated having more freedom than I did in California. My parents allowed me to let them know my plans for the day and be out and about, walking to where I wanted to be as long as I came home at the specified time. I had been nervous about eating sushi regularly but was delighted to discover that was only one aspect of Japanese cuisine. One of my favorite restaurants required people to take their shoes off upon entering, and small pits under the tables allowed you to sit comfortably on the floor. They had large placemats that served as menus with pictures and written information about items to order. I quickly got the hang of ordering one or two dishes at a time until I was full. My sister and I took a Japanese class over the first summer we lived there that culminated in an adventure I'll never forget!

We stayed with a couple in Japan for a short homestay. We took a bus ride with our classmates to a nearby city, met our host family, and saw where we would be staying for three days. They were as excited to practice their English with us as we were to practice our Japanese with them. We slept on tatami mats with pillows filled with rice. Tatami mats are made of bamboo or grass bound together to allow them to be folded and tucked away. The pillows were small and firm, and the rice moved around inside nicely. They were more comfortable than they first appeared.

As Japanese summers are filled with festivals, we got to walk in a parade during our homestay with some other Americans. There was a club that let our Japanese teacher know of different things students could participate in throughout the year, including the parade. The club had summer kimonos for my sister and me. Summer kimonos are similar to big lightweight robes wrapped firmly around the body and held in place with a cloth rope that matches it. We were to walk just a portion of the parade route but accidentally got separated from our group. We got caught up in waving and smiling at people watching the parade and seeing all the booths along the streets. Suddenly the group we were with did not match our kimonos! Our small amount of Japanese helped us haltingly ask the right questions to find our way back. We carefully walked against the stream of different groups in the parade until we saw someone dressed the same way we were. Luckily we found them just before everyone was inside the building changing back into their street clothes! It felt like it took ages, but in reality, it had been such a short time that no one realized we were missing. After the parade, we reunited with our host couple, and they made us a snack of corn on the cob before we went to bed that night. The gentleman of the house had an extensive garden, and our somewhat unusual bedtime snack came straight from their backyard and was proudly offered to us after being lightly boiled.

In a familiar scene during the same time of year as their first announcement, my parents sat my sister and me down to say we were moving back to the States. This time I saw the stress and worry on my parents' faces as they were talking to us, and I had enough maturity to decide to be helpful and kind as much as possible. We would return to California during my senior year of high school. I was entrenched even deeper in campus life by the time I was a senior, and I was heartbroken to say goodbye.

I had friends who understood what it was like to live in other countries and learn cultural norms different from those they'd known growing up. I knew I was saying goodbye to much of the freedom I had for exploring on my own. I would have to learn to drive again since Japan has the driver on the right side of the car and driving on the left side of the road. No more steaming bowls of ramen served alongside hot tea in mugs with no handles. I was not sad to say goodbye to the humid summers in Japan. I could handle it being hotter in California because it was a dry heat! At least this time, most of my friends had internet access. It would be easier to keep in touch through email. I also knew from hard-won experience that I could find adventure wherever I was as long as I kept my eyes open and my attitude right.

If you are facing a move of any distance, make the new spot feel homey as quickly as possible. Hang pictures on the walls and unpack music and movies to have a family night right away. Find out about local activities and make plans to drive around to find something interesting. The local library can be an excellent resource for finding community events and also the people to ask for restaurant recommendations or where to find the best park. Be open to new adventures. Freely try unfamiliar food and drinks because you might find new favorites! Accept invitations from new friends. At the heart of every successful move is diving into your new surroundings and making them feel like home. When you leave, you should feel like that place changed you a little bit and that you left a mark there, too.

ABOUT THE AUTHOR

"At the heart of every successful move is diving into your new surroundings and making it feel like home. When you leave, you should feel like that place changed you a little bit and that you left a mark there, too."

Melissa Calo-oy lives in Texas with her husband and their two boys. She is a pediatric nurse and a medical consultant at a daycare. She can quote extensively from animated and Marvel movies, along with knowing the parameters of vital signs for littles and the signs and symptoms of almost everything that should keep you home from daycare. In her spare time, Melissa loves to cook, share recipes with people, take naps, and is working on turning her front yard into a spot with something blooming each season. Her heart of hearts is that women would understand they have a purpose and a story to tell, even if they need a little help finding the time to put it into words. If you want to follow Melissa and her family's adventures as well as new projects she takes on, be sure to visit her website.

TEENAGE DISASTER

M y mom left my biological father when I was two years old. We moved from Nebraska to South Dakota and eventually Minnesota. Once in Minnesota, we moved around to various houses. First, we lived with my grandparents while Mom, my brother, and I got back on our feet. In second grade, we moved again, and I changed elementary schools. While I attended the new school, we moved around the area several times. We moved because the rent was raised or the landlords wanted to move into the house. Regardless of where we lived, Mom kept us in the same school. I was thankful to stay in the same school, knowing that I wouldn't have to leave my friends, or at least that is what I thought.

Mom's favorite house was in the country with enough land for our horses. It was close to my grandparents and semi-close to my high school. Mom would drive us to the bus stop, the farthest distance from the school, where the bus would pick up students. We had to get up early to be on the bus around 6:30 a.m. We would wait about five to fifteen minutes to board the bus, and then mom would turn around and race to work. Life was busy, running to the bus stop, going to school, taking care of the horses at night, shoveling snow, and doing homework I never completed on time. I am not sure how I stayed on the honor roll because I remember doing hours of makeup homework after each semester.

We dedicated our lives to the horses and used all our spare time to keep them alive and happy. We had to train, ride, groom, feed, and water them. We did not have any tractors or forklifts, so we did everything by hand. We got huge round hay bales from my grandfather at great prices. Then we would strip the hay bales apart layer by layer with pitchforks and carry as much as we could to the horses. When the hay bales would get small enough, we loaded the core onto our old gray Ford F150 pickup truck and drove to the farthest pasture to unroll it. It was always dark because mom didn't get off until late in the evening. Sometimes it was beautiful because we would lay in the hay and chat when we finished our work. We relaxed, looking up at the stars with snow sparkling all around us and listening to the horses munching their dinner. It's a unique sound that is hard to explain. As we sprawled out in the hay, we could see their ears perched forward, looking at us silly humans, laying on their meal. They would muzzle their way through to find the best and tastiest parts to eat first.

I enjoyed riding horses but didn't enjoy my lack of social life. When you're miles away from school out in the country, your friends are that much harder to reach. I always wanted to hang out with friends more, but I couldn't. My best friend would stay at my house for a week, and sometimes I could stay at her house for a week, and her family became my second family. For me, having a friend to hang out with was the most important thing in the whole world. She probably never knew it, but she lit up my life. The fact that she would stay at my house night after night was amazing

144

to me. It wasn't until I was a rebellious teenager that I learned I had to say goodbye to my friends and change schools again. Mom married a man she had been seeing for seven years.

We moved two and a half hours north to a house that Jeff and Mom were having renovated. The house was getting a significant face-lift and some added space. As we were packing, cleaning, and throwing stuff away, I tried to get out of it; I was never keen on working. My brother and I packed our rooms and helped my mom pack the rest of the house. Moving helped us purge our life of unnecessary items we had accumulated over the years. I remember throwing things away just because I was tired of packing. Sometimes mom would find items I shouldn't have thrown away and pull them out of the garbage. I didn't know then how moving was going to change my life.

The good thing about the move was I had less work to do. I cannot tell you how happy I was to be offloading that work to someone else. Jeff, my mom's newlywed husband, had tractors and a bobcat and worked full-time on the ranch. His entire livelihood revolved around the animals, which was great for mom. Every bit of time went to the farm. The animals needed feeding, watering, and everything else. Jeff had around a hundred head of cow-calf pairs, six bulls, and five horses, and mom had five horses. It was a big adjustment to go from a little hobby farm to a full-blown ranch, but we were adjusting to so much more than that.

We did not live with Jeff before they married, so moving in with him was a *huge* adjustment for all of us. I was never a clean person, and my disorganization became a problem. My room was in the loft, and there were no closets, curtains, or drapes. There was nowhere to put my stuff; I couldn't put it away, and I couldn't hang it up, so it got splashed around the room. The loft was open to the floor below, and even though I craved privacy, there was very little of it. I was told to clean my room, but the only thing I could do was make piles of things I had to go through each time I needed something. I gave up on keeping my room clean; what's the point when you can't put away your things?

I also left a great school with teachers that I was close to, and I left my best friend behind. Living outside a tiny town with less than three hundred people, the new school had a class size of *fourteen kids*. I didn't want to move into a class that had been close-knit since kindergarten. I was enrolled in that tiny school right up until the very first day of school. I was filled with dread and was so upset. I already had no social life, and I didn't want to try to join such a small school as an outsider. When the first day of school came, mom agreed to send me to the school in the next town. At least there were over sixty kids in that class, and I had more hope of fitting into at least one group.

Mom got a job in the same town, and I rode with her every morning. She worked early in the morning, giving me about 45 minutes before school started to talk with other kids who got there early, and an hour and a half after school before I would have to return to the ranch. With my extra time, I planned to create some new friendships.

I kept asking my mom if I could hang out with kids around school, but often the answer was "No." She wanted me to have well-educated friends, but we moved into a fairly low-income area, and people didn't have the best education. I felt like I was in a box and couldn't get out; I needed some air. I am a fighter, and holding me down does not work; the tighter you hold on to me, the more it makes me struggle to get away. I get it - my mom enjoyed having me home, but I needed people outside the home. I needed friends. Being stuck in a box changed when I got a job. I worked at a nursing home and saved enough money to buy a car in cash.

It was a red Pontiac Grand Prix. I loved that car! It was freedom and my ticket to creating some friends and the life I wanted. It felt like I was fighting my parents for what I wanted, and I decided that if they wouldn't help me or work with me, I would get it myself. As I started paying for my clothes, car, and phone, I began to think I could stay out for however long I wanted, even though I had a curfew at 9:00 p.m. It was a tense time. Mom and Jeff tried the whole "as long as you're under my roof" speech, but that didn't work. I quit asking my mom to hang out with people and just did it. I didn't come home by curfew; sometimes, I didn't come home until 2:00 a.m. They couldn't take my car away because I bought it.

Whose kids are allowed to stay out after hours when their family doesn't know where they are? The kids who have absent parents. I started hanging out with these kids, and they were not the greatest influences, but hey, I had friends. My grades suffered. I went from the honor roll to barely passing classes. Thankfully, I eventually got to know my teachers the same way I knew them before. I had some incredible teachers who impacted my life significantly. Mr. Houseman is the reason that I got into graphic design and the reason that I love art, and Mr. Nissen is the reason that I continued to be involved in art.

Since the beginning of the move, as I was told "No" when I wanted to go out, I started to keep my family at arm's length. They were great people but were trying to adjust to a new area and family dynamic themselves. It was hard for my family to see that I was struggling. My brother had gone to college, and I was alone. I needed to have some fun, and I wanted to have more fun than in a regulated (you have to act this way to be accepted) way. I wanted to laugh, go to concerts, discuss books with other people, relate to people, and have freedom.

My mom loves me sooo much. I don't think anyone else on earth will ever love me as much as my mom loves me, and I know she loves my brother just as much. I felt terrible for pushing them away, but sooner or later, you have to cut the umbilical cord.

It can be challenging when you're a teen who feels trapped in your situation. But understand that your parents have the best intentions at heart. Instead of putting all your effort into rebelling, focus on your future. It's only a few years away. If you focus on finishing high school and setting yourself up for college, you can finish on time and move on.

To the parents with a rebellious child, take time for that child because their behavior is telling you they are unhappy. If your child is staying in their room all the time and not coming out, and they don't want to go on family vacations or trips, they might be depressed. It's essential to find out why they are depressed and help them. Try to do things they like and talk with them. It's crucial to ensure that you don't become angry that they are depressed or that the life you cultivated doesn't fit them exactly.

We are all people, and teenagers are just like other people. They have their own ideas, and it is vital to pay attention to their preferences. Chances are, if you're a strong-headed parent, your child will have a strong head and need you to listen. Just because most of the family is happy with the things they always do or how things are at home doesn't mean everyone is happy. Each child is different, each teen is different, and each grows up to be an individual adult. They must have room to grow and explore, and by listening and working together, each family member can grow to be the best person they can be.

About the Author

"It was a big adjustment to go from a little hobby farm to a full-blown ranch, but we were adjusting to so much more than that."

Kerry Anderson is a graphic designer who loves to inspire people through visual designs. She is passionate about exploring new experiences, traveling to national parks, and backpacking. Kerry enjoys spending time going on any adventure with dear friends and family. Kerry strives to live life in full color, be vibrant, and enjoy every day.

Acknowledgments

Thank you to each author in this book! Your willingness to openly share your story with the world will make a lasting impact. Thank you for going on this journey with me, pouring your time into this book, courageously choosing to show up in this world, and speaking encouragement to those who are going through a move.

Thank you to my family and friends who encourage the big dreams God has gifted to me to bring forth.

Thank you, Erika Harston Noll, for coming alongside me with the editing of this book. Your encouragement, ideas, and suggestions were abundantly helpful.

Thank you, Britte Osiek, for your flexibility, swift work, and ability to take my vague descriptions of graphic ideas and create beautiful images with them.

Thank you, Meggan Larson, for breaking through your glass ceilings and showing me that I could do the same.

Bonus Course

If you are ready for *even more* content related to moving to a new area, check out the BONUS COURSE!

READ THE REST OF THE SERIES

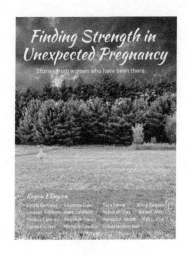

COMING SOON

A Shy Girl's Guide to Making Friends After A Move:
The Art of Conversation

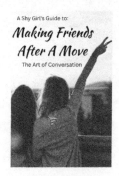

Jump on the waiting list and get notified as soon as the book comes
out!

ONE LAST THING

Reviews are important for any book on Amazon. If you would click five stars on when you visit the link below at your convenience, that will ensure that I can continue to produce more books. Without stars or reviews, you would not have found this book. Please take just a few seconds of your time to show your support by leaving a rating.
Thank you so much!

Leave a review here:

Sincerly,
Kaycia Ellingsen

Made in the USA
Monee, IL
30 December 2023

49433767R00092